BIBLICAL LEADERSHIP

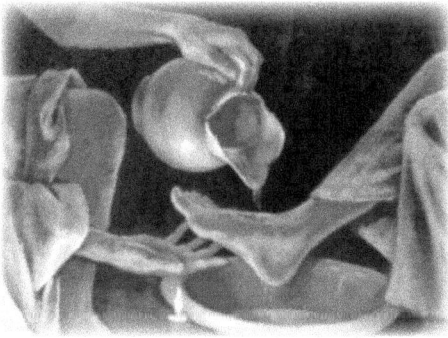

BIBLICAL LEADERSHIP

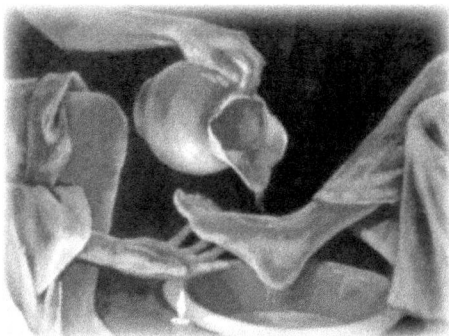

BECOMING
A DIFFERENT KIND OF LEADER

KEN COLLIER & MATT WILLIAMS

AMBASSADOR INTERNATIONAL
GREENVILLE, SOUTH CAROLINA & BELFAST, NORTHERN IRELAND

Biblical Leadership:
Becoming a Different Kind of Leader

Cover design & page layout by A & E Media — Paula Shepherd

Hardcover ISBN: 978-1-64960-221-3
Paperback ISBN: 978-1-93230-721-4
Ebook ISBN: 978-1-62020-461-0

Published by the Ambassador Group

Ambassador Emerald International
427 Wade Hampton Blvd.
Greenville, SC 29609
USA
www. emeraldhouse.com

and

Ambassador Publications Ltd.
Providence House
Ardenlee Street
Belfast BT6 8QJ
Northern Ireland
www. ambassador-productions.com

The colophon is a trademark of Ambassador

From Ken Collier:

My portion of this book is dedicated to my wonderful family. Mardi, you are just right! You have taught me to know God by being in the same place every morning, seeking to know His character. Matt, Evan, Aaron and Natalie, you have made fatherhood a complete "joy" and never a "grief". You have made me a rich man. Kelly, Natalie Sue and Naomi, I would have chosen each one of you as my own, if the choice had been mine.

From Matt Williams:

This book is dedicated to my wife and five children. Donna, you are the most consistent Christian I know, having a hunger and thirst for God's Word and a loving compassion for all those around you. Kevin, Valarie, Kari, Joy and Chad, you have made and continue to make me a blessed father. I am so thankful for your heart for God and others. Holly, Tim and Adam, you are a special addition to our family and lives.

Acknowledgements
FROM KEN COLLIER

- To my camp family at The WILDS, in whom I have studied these principles all day, every day. No one could have more godly brothers and sisters.

- To Craig Krueger for bringing the order out of the chaos so that God may receive greater glory.

- To my secretary, Caroline Floyd, who always does the "next right thing" when it comes to ministry and help.

- To Ken Hay and Jim Berg, whom I am proud to say are my mentors.

Acknowledgements
FROM MATT WILLIAMS

- To the wonderful staff at Tri-City Ministries for the many years of encouragement and godly example.

- To my co-laborer Craig Krueger for all of his labor of love in editing.

- To my secretary, Susan Wilson, for her countless hours of help in all of my projects.

- To my friend, Ron Raymer, for his artwork used on the cover.

- To all of the faculty, staff members and students that I have had the privilege of seeing these principles incorporated into their lives over the years.

Foreword

There are many types of leaders. I have seen them in the business world, in government, in the home, and in the local church. Sorry to say, many times the leadership I have observed has been totally contrary to what the Bible teaches. Many leaders are focused on what they can *get from* their positions of authority, rather than on what they can *give to* the works in which they are involved. Jesus, in Matthew 20, said that "the son of man came not to be ministered unto, but to minister, and to give his life a ransom for many." This is the kind of leadership the Bible talks about—this is servant leadership.

I am very thankful that Ken Collier and Matt Williams have taken time to put these biblical leadership principles into print. I am also glad that these two men have verified the truth of these principles by living them in front of me and many others. I have known both Ken and Matt for over 20 years. They have practiced biblical leadership in their homes, in their churches, and in their communities. I wish everyone could know these two men the way I know them. However, reading this book will help you to understand what makes them servant leaders. Whether you get to meet Ken and Matt personally or not, you will be able to catch a glimpse of their heart in each chapter of *Biblical Leadership*.

When you read this book, I trust you will purpose in your heart to live it as well. You will notice many references to Scripture. The best book on leadership is the Bible. Ken and Matt present passages of Scripture that talk specifically about leadership. They help us learn how to apply these truths in the day in which we live. Please purpose in your heart, as you read this book, to practice the biblical principles that are communicated.

Leadership is a privilege. Leadership also requires responsibility. We need biblical leaders who are people of integrity and humility. I pray this book will help you, me, and many in the generations to come to be the biblical leaders God wants us all to be.

Carl D. Herbster
Pastor, Tri-City Ministries

Table of Contents

Preface: A Leader Like No Other 1

Section I. Christ Our Example
   1.   A Different Head 5

Section II. What Does it Mean to be a Different Kind of Leader?
   2.   A Different Heart. 19
   3.   A Different Goal. 31
   4.   A Different Authority 41
   5.   A Different Leadership. 49
   6.   A Different Spirit. 59
   7.   A Different Love 67

Section III. How Can I be a Different Kind of Leader?
   8.   Different Choices. 83
   9.   Different Attitudes and Actions 91
  10.   A Different Way of Handling Problems. 103
  11.   A Different Home 119
  12.   Different Relationships. 129
Conclusion: Attracted to Jesus Christ 145

Appendix 1.
   1.   Case Studies. 149

Appendix 2.
   1.   For Husbands: Serving My Wife. 155
   2.   For Wives: Serving My Husband 159
   3.   For Parents: Serving My Children 163
   4.   For Children and Teens: Serving My Parents 165

Introductory Note

Biblical Leadership was brought about by a different kind of authorship. We are writing on the same topic, presenting the same biblical truth, yet the Lord has brought us through very different sets of life experiences. For instance, Ken grew up in Bible-believing churches, but Matt was twenty-four years old when the Lord brought him from formal religion to a personal relationship with Himself. We have collaborated on every chapter, but since many of our explanations and illustrations reflect our different life experiences, we thought it would be less confusing for the reader if we identified the primary writer of each chapter.

May the Lord bless you as you become a *Different Kind of Leader!*

KEN COLLIER & MATT WILLIAMS

Preface

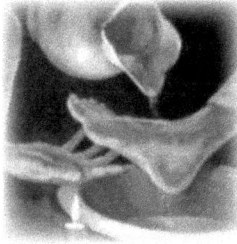

A LEADER LIKE NO OTHER

L eadership is influence, so the accepted definition goes. *Influence is the ability to move another person in a direction you believe is important.* By any definition, Jesus Christ was a leader like no other! He has influenced me! Has He influenced you? Has He moved you in the direction He counts important in His plan of the ages? Have you become a leader who follows?

Jesus Christ was the greatest leader the world has ever known because He was the greatest follower the world has ever known. He had a sharply focused view of exactly what His Father desired of Him. No trial, no deprivation, no conflict, no misunderstanding, and no death threat made Him swerve from following the will of His Father. What a leader! What a Follower!

Although those terms may sound contradictory, this dynamic balance is what God desires in our lives. He desires a leader who blazes a clear trail because his eye is on *the* Leader. God desires churches which walk the straight path because the leadership does not get lost on rabbit trails; rather, the leaders pursue the path of the Just One. God wants Christian school leaders in junior and senior classes who—because they have a grasp of what God desires for their school—shatter the mold of what teenagers normally are.

The primary quality of a godly leader is that he follows Someone who is stronger than he is, wiser than he is, more discerning than he is, and more in control of circumstances than he is. A godly *leader*, whether a parent, teacher, supervisor, deacon, business leader, or student body officer, *excels at following* Someone to a greater degree than others around him do. How unlike this pattern is from the modern view of a leader as one who is great because he chooses a direction and consults only himself and his own resources!

God's plan calls for a different kind of leader. His plan calls for someone who loves to be under authority and proves it by following God alone. His plan demands a leader who realizes that his greatest duty is to follow another. This is the leader who will make a difference at home, at school, at church and at work.

A Godly leader must be
DIFFERENT ON PURPOSE!

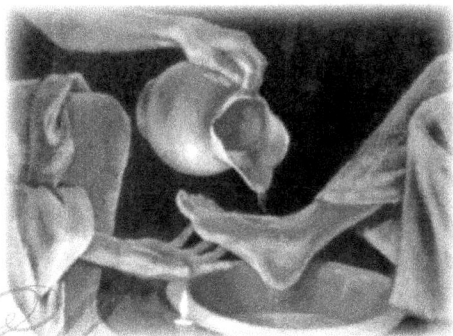

Christ, our Example

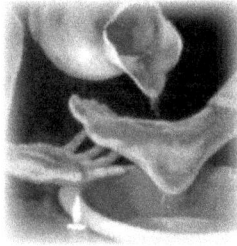

Chapter 1

A DIFFERENT HEAD: JESUS CHRIST

by Ken Collier

A Very Different Idea: A Leader Is a Servant

I was stunned, but this was exactly what I had been looking for. The speaker had just given a challenge about Abraham's servant in Genesis 24, and what he said was like a flash of lightning suddenly illuminating a nighttime scene. It was a simple enough concept. Verse 2 reads, *And Abraham said unto his eldest **servant** of his house, that ruled over all that he had...* This was a revelation to me. This man was called *his eldest servant*, but he was obviously a good leader. As a matter of fact, he *ruled over all that he had!* This man, capable of being a servant, was the kind of man Abraham chose to be the leader of his household! Is it possible that being a servant helps qualify one to be a leader? If the good leader is a good leader because he is a good servant and a good follower, that would be different from the commonly accepted profile of a leader.

Wanting to know more, I spent several very intense and exciting personal sessions studying this man who was a servant, yet a leader. He was a man of action; he had his master's goods in his hands; yet he was very careful to hear and carry out his master's instructions carefully. He was a man of faith, expecting God to help him find the ideal wife for Isaac. The predominant characteristic he was looking for in this girl was something that he knew would be manifested by her willingness to draw water for ten thirsty camels! That is no small task! This man was a servant looking for another servant! Rebekah, a willing camel-waterer, was the servant for whom Eliezer was looking. As testimony to the Lord's blessing on his mission, Abraham's servant gave the secret of his success, saying, *I being in the way, the Lord led me to the house of my master's brethren* (Genesis 24: 27b). The secret of his success can be the secret of ours.

Oh, to be in that fellowship of servants who are *in the way* when God wants to get His work accomplished in the lives of others. Willing servants are not *in the way* for bad, but are literally *on the way* of duty when God wants to bring direction and blessing to others. It seems that the best way to live life is to be *on the way* and *in the way*. If the Lord wants to direct people toward becoming like Christ—and He does—then maybe in some small way He could use us if we are willing, prepared and available to be *in the way*. I remember thinking that, whether I was in a position of formal leadership or not, it was impossible to go wrong while being a servant to others! I have pursued this goal imperfectly through the years, yet the blessings that have come from attempting to serve by being *in the way* have been immense! Has that been your experience? Have you been *in God's way* and *on God's way* to the extent that He is using you to lead others closer to Himself?

Don't just stand there!
GET IN THE WAY!

Looking Back

Testing the principle of **leaders being servants** in my own past, I recalled the people who led me, those who had the greatest impact in my life. Though they were very influential in my life, not one of them would be considered extraordinary by the world's standards. I remember a Sunday school teacher who loved our rambunctious class of junior boys. He was a factory worker who actually seemed to enjoy taking fifteen junior boys out camping. Around that campfire I learned the lessons of sacrifice and love from a good leader. I do not remember his spoken lessons, but his leadership influenced me.

There was also a cafeteria worker in a public school whose influence on my life continues. She was my Sunday school teacher when no on else would volunteer. I remember a lay youth director who may have been short on technique and knowledge, but he was long on serving and loving teenagers. His acts of servanthood—even while he was being treated unkindly, his teaching was being made fun of, his activities were being boycotted—became an unforgettable example of a *leader* who *served*. Dozens of other people crowd my mind. Some were the adults in my life. Some were my peers. Each one was my leader. Each one influenced me by his or her spirit of serving. Each one influenced me in the direction that was important to him or her, which happened to be God's direction. Each one led me in a manner greatly different from the confident, assertive, dramatic leadership that is revered today. None of them were charismatic-type leaders who were influential with thousands. Each one was *in the way* when God desired to teach me the life of Christ. Each of them led me in a simple, forthright, yet distinctly *different* way.

A Different Kind of Leader!

This book is for men and women who make, or desire to make, an impact on others in the Body of Christ. Your biography, like those of the servant-leaders who have affected my life, is not likely to end up in a large Christian publication, much less in the *Wall Street Journal*, but you do find yourself in some position of leadership. Did you get your position of leadership because you have formal training in the field? That is possible. Perhaps you became a leader in your church, your school, or your ministry because you have acquired a storehouse of experience. Chances are that experience came on the field of battle. You learned as you went. Perhaps you are where you are because no one else would volunteer for the position. Maybe you lead because you signed on and automatically became the leader, ready or not! It is obvious that you cannot be a parent, a teacher, a preacher, a Sunday school officer, a Christian school administrator, a deacon, or a youth sponsor without functioning as a leader. It comes with the package. It is part of the deal. We may be the reluctant leaders, but, whether we love it, like it, or sigh heavily, we are the leaders God has chosen to use, and God gets His work done through us! God is getting His work done with willing servants, average people who are good followers of Christ. Amazing, isn't it?

...Meet the Perfect Leader!

Have you met the perfect servant-leader? Surely you have, for Jesus Christ is the perfect leader. This book is for people who desire to be *different* in leadership even as Christ was *different!* It is for people who, knowing Christ as Savior, will honestly check the type of leadership they are exercising in all of the various roles of life to see if it is modeled after the leadership of Jesus Christ. He is the leader who served! He is the servant who leads! After all, when Christ came to earth, His leadership appeared so *different*, so *unlike others*, that it was startling and puzzling to everyone, including the men who lived and walked with Him each day. His disciples were so amazed at the mighty power of the One who was their Teacher that they begged Him to allow them to call down fire on the men who would not receive Him. Christ, however, being the leader and yet the humble servant, rebuked His disciples for their impetuousness.

The religious Zealots admired His power, yet they came to despise His leadership. They wanted a militant warrior-leader who would cast off the bonds of Rome. They wanted someone who would exert his power and push the Romans out of Israel. Instead they found a man who *went about doing good*. Make no mistake, He will be the warrior-leader someday! Those who rejected the servant-leader will be in for a shock. The religious leaders rejected His leadership for He refused to play the power and popularity games and refused to perform miracles on command. But God the Father knew that the influence of His Son's leadership would bring salvation to His friends and His enemies, those near and those far off. The *difference* in the way Christ lived and led people moved the Father to observe, *This is my Beloved Son, in whom I am well pleased; hear ye him (Matthew 17:5).*

Christ Explains His Leadership

Please read the following brief passages:

And he came to Capernaum: and being in the house he asked them, What was it that ye disputed among yourselves by the way? But they held their peace: for by the way they had disputed among themselves, who should be the greatest. And He sat down, and called the twelve, and saith unto them, If any man desire to be first, the same shall be last of all, and servant of all (Mark 9:33-35).

But Jesus called them to Him, and saith unto them, Ye know that they which are accounted to rule over the Gentiles exercise lordship over them; and their great ones exercise authority upon them, But so shall it not be among you: but whosoever will be great among you, shall be your minister: And whosoever of you will be the chiefest, shall be servant of all. For even the Son of Man came not to be ministered unto, but to minister, and to give his life a ransom for many (Mark 10:42-45).

Follow the Leader

Do you realize, *Christian leader,* that you follow the greatest Leader in the history of the world? In light of the simple definition of leadership, "the ability of one to influence another in a direction he thinks is important," have you not been influenced by Jesus Christ? Without His leadership we would be without God and without hope in this world and the next! We could still be leading others, and we could still be being led, but it would be away from God, not towards God. Christ led us to the Father. *For when we were yet without strength, in due time Christ died of the ungodly* (Romans 5:6).

Given all the military leaders, political leaders, founders of countries, discoverers, and the like, nobody ever made as much difference for all time as did Christ! He is the Leader of all the leaders, and you are enrolled in His instruction course. He has taken His time to teach us how to lead others. Here are the principles used by the greatest Leader, the One you and I are to be following. Honestly evaluate the leadership positions you presently hold. Honestly consider the type of leadership position you would hold if you could. Would the following traits mark your leadership…as they mark Christ's?

He did not selfishly dominate others

In Mark 10 Christ set His disciples down in order to gain their full attention. He outlined a clear picture of what His leadership would be and what it would not be. The Bible states in Mark 10:42-43a, *But Jesus called them to Him, and saith unto them, Ye know that they which are accounted to rule **over** the Gentiles exercise lordship **over** them; and their **great ones** exercise authority **upon** them. But so shall it **not be among you**….*[1] In this passage, the prepositions tell the story (see emphasized words). Leadership that is not like Christ's will endeavor to get its way by dominating, bullying, or manipulating others. Christ simply followed His Father's truth and led us to do the same. Gentile leadership emphasizes using a position or authority to get what one wants. Christ, our leader, never used His position or authority to selfishly rule over us. Christ never selfishly dominated or manipulated others. Are there Christian leaders who use the power of their leadership to dominate people, to manipulate people, or to get their own way? Yes, but this is not Christ's way. This is the ungodly way, the way of those without Christ.

He ministered

The Greek word translated "servant" is *diakonos,* from which we get our word *deacon.* Christ was the ever-vigilant *minister* who would always do the next thing that met the genuine needs of others. My

[1] Emphasis mine

particular focus in using word *minister* is on this diligent seeking to help. Whether He was healing the eyes of a man born blind or rebuking the self-righteous religious leaders of His day, Christ gave each one what he genuinely needed! Christ invested Himself *on purpose* to bring others to a right relationship with His Father. He was a minister like this world has never known. As stated in John 21: 25, *And there are also many other things which Jesus did, the which, if they should be written every one, I suppose that even the world itself could not contain the books that should be written. Amen.*

The great ones in God's estimation do not dominate; they minister. Everything Christ did was in the context of ministering, doing the next thing that would genuinely benefit the life of another. He knew what to do next. Are we using our position of leadership to do the next thing that meets the needs of the people we serve? Is the notable thing about your leadership the fact that you know what to do next to meet the needs of the people whom you are called to lead?

He served

As I am using the term *serve,* the focus is on how the leader helps to make the Master successful in the lives of others.

This is the key point in the ability of Christ to lead men: He served. He served His Father. He served you and me. He was the King, with all of the accompanying power, yet He used His power to serve us. Christ says in Mark 10:44, *And whosoever of you will be the chiefest, shall be servant of all.* From the greatest leader who has ever walked the planet comes one of the most startling statements ever made: "If you want to be the first in position or influence," says Christ, "you must become a servant of all."

What is a servant? A servant is one who gets joy and delight in the success of his master in any endeavor. A true servant in biblical times, often a bond slave through his own choice, would live his entire life dominated by doing that which brought honor and delight to another person, namely, his own master. Success, to a bondservant, would be making his master successful in any pursuit the master chose. A servant's day was dominated by his submission to his master in at least two main areas:

1) He was responsive to the will of another.

2) He was responsive to the needs of others.

Jesus Christ was the model leader because He did what He commanded other godly leaders to do: He served! As Christian leaders in any realm, do we use our power to serve? If we would lead like Christ, we must be practiced at serving, not dominating people.

He sacrificed

*For even the Son of man came **not to be ministered unto,** but to **minister, and to give his life** a ransom for many* (Mark 10:45). Christ was not a taker in this life; He was a giver. A stroll through Scripture will prove this point emphatically. He sacrificed in every area. He left Heaven's glory for earth's sorrows. He was born in a stable, not in a palace. He had no house, although the least of His creatures have houses, dens, or nests. He was often weary because of the demands on His time and energy. He was in constant demand by the multitudes desiring His help. He even laid down His life willingly to repay a debt that was not His. His whole life was spent in sacrifice for the needs of others.

Would you want to follow a leader who, far from being self-serving and pompous, is always sacrificial when others have genuine needs? Yes, you would. People in your home, church, workplace, or school would love to follow such a leader, too! He *gave His life a ransom for many.* He sacrificed even to the point of a cross-death (Philippians 2: 3-11)! His love for His Father was great! His love for us was great! He sacrificed! Would we continually do the sacrificial thing for the ones God has called us to lead? Would we do the thing that is most sacrificial?

Being a *different kind of leader* means following the model of leadership laid out by the greatest leader who ever lived. We should accept no other alternative types of leadership. If we desire to be like Christ, we must learn to lead by serving!

In short, if you are going to be a leader like our Leader, the Lord Jesus Christ, you are choosing, not to selfishly dominate, but to sacrificially serve those whom you lead.

Surprise the world:
FOLLOW THE LEADER!

Summary
- A biblical leader is a servant

    ◦ Illustrated in Scripture Genesis 24, 27.

    ◦ Illustrated through life examples.

    ◦ Illustrated through the perfect leader, Jesus Christ.

- A biblical leader explained by Christ

    ◦ Mark 9:33-35

    ◦ Mark 10:42-45

    ◦ He did not dominate with his actions.

    ◦ He led by ministering.

    ◦ He ministered by serving.

    ◦ He served by sacrificing.

- Leadership is following our leader Jesus Christ.

For Consideration and Action
- Do you consider yourself a servant-leader who has been given the responsibility to rule or a ruler leader who occasionally serves?

- Who are the five greatest servants who have influenced your life to this point? Is there a common trait that you need to be aware of and emulate?

- What would have to change in order for you to be "in the way," that is, on the way as an instrument of God's blessing to those around you? What sacrifice of time and resources would it require?

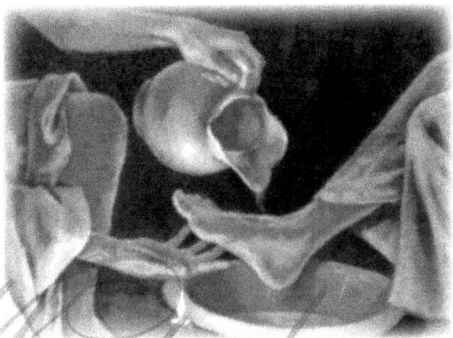

What does it mean to be a different kind of leader?

Chapter 2

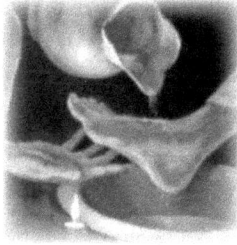

A DIFFERENT HEART

by Matt Williams

S ome years ago I spent two months in basic training for the United States Army at Fort Leonard Wood, Missouri. Basic training was tough! Not only are February and March a very cold time of the year in the Midwest, but I also had a drill sergeant who seemed determined to push the stereotype of his profession beyond tough to just plain cruel! I found out later that our company had needed one more drill sergeant; so, just before my group of recruits arrived, the officers took a private who had just graduated from basic training two days before and slapped sergeant strips on his arm. This was my drill sergeant. I don't know if he was taking out on us the frustrations from his own basic training, but this new sergeant was ruthless! We would be running up and down the hills of southwest Missouri with our weapons over our heads, and he would grab weapons from different recruits and beat them over the head for motivation. Or if someone wasn't doing as well as he expected, he'd kick him and knock him to the ground. It was not a pleasant experience!

It seemed like the only enjoyment we were having was at dinner time. We would sit around the table in the dining hall and gripe about our drill sergeant. Now that was fun! It was fun for everyone...except Eddie. I'll never forget him. Eddie was a little guy who would respond to our comments with statements like, "Aw, guys, he's just trying to make good soldiers out of us." I would be thinking, "Eddie! Did you see what he did today?" But he would go on with something like, "Guys he's just trying to get us ready for combat duty." He was always saying something positive about the drill sergeant. Guess what. Two things happened. First, when Eddie was around, we stopped complaining. He was a positive influence on all of us, keeping our conversation somewhat uplifting and positive. But something even stranger happened: after a while, I'd begin to say to myself, "Oh, he's just trying to make good soldiers out of us," or "He's just trying to get us ready for combat duty." Eddie's attitude was contagious! I actually started believing it after a while since I had heard it so often from Eddie. He was influencing me and others in a greater fashion than we realized.

A Difference Noticed by Others

Eddie was also different in other areas. He was always reading his Bible. Guys would hide it from him or even put pornography inside of it. He would find his Bible, throw the pictures away and begin to read. Eddie was different on purpose, and he greatly influenced my life. I am certain that he got as frustrated as the rest of us did with many of the methods used in our preparation for duty, but he had a bigger purpose in life. As Christians, we, too, have a bigger purpose in life, and we have the privilege of influencing others' lives for Jesus Christ. The question is, what kind of influence are we on those around us?

Our Privilege—Being Salt and Light

Scripture tells us that we have the responsibility and the privilege to be salt and light. *Ye are the salt of the earth; but if the salt have lost his savour, wherewith shall it be salted? It is thenceforth good for nothing, but to be cast out, and to be trodden under foot of men. Ye are the light of the world. A city that is set on a hill cannot be hid. Neither do men light a candle, and put it under a bushel, but on a candlestick; and it giveth light onto all that are in the house. Let your light so shine before men, that they may see your good works, and glorify your Father which is in heaven* (Matthew 5:13-16).

We are to be the salt of the earth. Let's think about the many uses of salt for just a moment. It *seasons* food, giving it more taste. It *preserves* food to make it last longer. I have even heard of putting salt on wounds to help *heal* them from infection. Making practical application to our lives, we must ask ourselves whether we are seasoning the environments we live in each day. Are our homes better homes, our neighborhoods better neighborhoods, our work places more like God's ideal because we are there? Is the cause of Christ preserved and promoted because we are there? Are wounds being healed in lives because of our testimony and daily presence? It is our privilege to be salt.

We are also to be the light of the world. We should be illuminating the way and leading people out of darkness. Light is that which penetrates and dispels darkness. Scripture tells us that God is light and that God's Word is light. The character of light is to reveal reality. It allows us to appreciate what is pure and to correct what is impure. The opposite of light is darkness, which obscures, deceives, and harbors impurity. An interesting thought is that Jesus says, *I am the Light* (John 8:12). Both the sun and moon provide light, but the sun is the actual source of the light; the moon then reflects that same light. Jesus Christ, the Son of God is the actual source of the light. Our responsibility is to be reflectors, transmitting the true Light of the Son into the darkness around us.

This passage also contains a sobering reality: *But if the salt have lost his savor, …It is thenceforth good for nothing, but to be cast out, and to be trodden under foot of men* (Matthew 5:13). If we just want to be average, just want to be ones that go along with the crowd and be just like everyone else, we're really good for nothing. We are to be salt and light to a lost and dying world. Are you being a light to others where you are?

There was a girl in our Christian school years ago who greatly influenced us all. She was there for only one year before her dad was transferred to another city, but her influence remained long after she left. Her name was Cindy, but the students called her "Sunshine." It was a fitting name because she brightened up the environment wherever she went. Her smile, her countenance, her love for the Lord and others shone brightly in every situation.

This is not a quality unique to teenage girls. I think of Ed Brammeier in our church. Although well into his retirement years—hearing aid and all!—his energetic, cheerful, and positive attitude has led some to call him one of Tri-City's oldest teenagers. His positive attitude makes him an encouragement to people and a promoter of that which is good within the church. His experience and solid Scriptural foundation makes him a valuable counselor, and even a discerner of good and evil, as he serves as a deacon.

I trust that each of us takes seriously our responsibility to be salt and light.

Make a difference:
BE SALT AND LIGHT!

Two Key Reminders

As we consider being a different kind of leader, there are two key principles to consider.

In order to make a difference, you have to be different

Being average just won't work if you intend to be God's agent of change in your situation. *Average* is being more concerned about what everyone else *thinks* of me than about what God *expects* of me. Galatians 1:10 clearly challenges us on this point: "For do I now persuade men, or God? Or do I seek to please men? For if I yet pleased men, I should not be the servant of Christ." *Average* is trying to live my life for *myself* instead of seeking to obey *God*. *Average* is doing what I *feel* like doing instead of doing what I *know* to be God's commands. God lovingly but firmly calls us to choose: "If ye love me, keep my commandments" (John 14:15).

One of the things that surprised me early in my Christian life was that I saw Christians often handling problems the same way that non-Christians did. Their solutions were based on their feelings or on their own reasoning. But we can't say we weren't warned—God's Word has plenty to say on that topic: *There is a way which seemeth right unto a man, but the end thereof are the ways of death* (Proverbs 14:12). I think this must be especially important, because, two chapters later, God says it again, word for word, in Proverbs 16:25. As believers, our responses must be based on God's Word if we are going to make a difference in the lives of others. We don't have to look for ways to be different. If we just obey God's Word, we *will* be different.

You can't change the quality of something by adding more of the same

Consider a glass of unsweetened iced tea. If you want sweetened tea, you won't get it by adding more ice. Plunking in another type of tea bag won't help. Adding more water or boiling some off won't make it any sweeter. And certainly waiting will not change it. The only way to make a difference is to add something that wasn't there before.[2]

When I speak of changing the "quality" of something, I am referring to qualitative change as different from quantitative change. *Qualitative change* is adding or deleting something so that the nature—the type of stuff, whether iced tea or godly attitudes—of the mix is changed. *Quantitative change* merely alters the proportions of what is already there. Nothing new is added.

Now consider your situation. Whether in a church, a family, a school, or a work environment, if you want to make a difference, you have to be different. *Different* means "not the same, distinct, unlike most others." It comes from the root *dis* which means "apart" and *ferre* which means "to bring." To be different is to be apart and to be distinctive. If we are like everyone else, blending into each situation, having as our central motivation to please those around us, then we are not being different on purpose. We are not changing the quality of the situation around us because we are just adding more of the same. Have you ever watched a group of teens? They may wear the same clothes, the same type of shoes, and, most of the time, the same name brands. They may tie or button exactly the same. This is not necessarily bad, but often their lives depict that they are carbon copies of others.

Remember playing the game, "Follow the Leader" when you were a child? Well, that's what life is all about: seeking to follow our leader, Jesus Christ. There's something distinctively different about following the Supreme Leader. We will be obedient to His will; our lives will be shaped by His wishes. *By this we know that we love the children of God, when we love God, and keep his commandments. For this is the love of God, that we keep his commandments: and his commandments are not grievous* (I John 5: 2-3). If we can follow our Leader and fit in with the present situation, that

---

[2] Based on, Jim Berg, *Changed into His Image*, Bob Jones University Press, 1999.

is okay. If we need to be different from what is happening around us, then let's be bold and not just add more of the same.

You will be different because of your different purpose in life.
BE DIFFERENT BECAUSE OF FOLLOWING CHRIST!

What is Leadership?

We are bombarded with leadership books, tapes, CDs, seminars, and conferences. But what is leadership? As I have asked that question over the years, I have heard many definitions such as being "the person in charge," "the guy at the top," or "one who makes things happen." A dictionary might give leadership a more generic definition, such as "to provide direction or guidance." But actually leadership is much more than all of these.

After years of study, books, tapes, and seminars, I have come to a one-word definition for leadership: *influence*. It is *the ability to influence someone* in a *direction* that you *think* is important. Isn't that what Matthew 5:13-16, the passage on salt and light, tells us? Every one of us is a leader. And we all have the same opportunity to influence others in our homes, neighborhoods, jobs, churches, and schools. What effect are we having on those around us? Are we a positive or a negative influence? Is ours a godly influence—showing others Christ through our lives? Are we living illustrations of the Christian life being the superior way of life?

Types of Leadership

While working for The J.C. Penny Company some years ago I had the privilege of attending a leadership seminar. The presenter was going to discuss four different types of leadership. I was excited about *learning* the four types, but I was even more excited about *using* these in my Christian life. The first type was the *positional leader*, someone who is a leader because of his or her position. Every one of us has positional leadership. You may have a responsibility on your job, and because of that position you are over others. You may have a position in your church and are considered a part of the leadership team. You may be a junior in high school, and, because of your position as a junior, you are a leader. Whatever the grade, whatever the church position, or whatever the job, just because of that position you become a leader to others. But the seminar leader taught that, although positional leadership is a type of leadership, it is not the best type.

He next described a second type of leadership. It's what I'm going to call *personality leadership*. It's leadership that results because someone enjoys being around you. Your personality is one that he or she enjoys, and that fact gives you opportunity to influence that person. I remember a few summers ago we were at camp. We had brought 200 junior and junior-high campers from Kansas City to a camp thirteen hours away. That's quite an adventure just getting there on five old, yellow school buses! When we finally arrived, we had a great camp. As I watched some of those counselors whose campers followed them everywhere, I saw personality leadership in action. Whatever those counselors did, the campers did. Wherever those counselors were, the campers were. It seemed like these counselors would fall over several of their campers every time they turned around. The campers stayed close because they just enjoyed being around their counselors. They liked them. They looked up to them. That is personality leadership. What a wonderful illustration of using acceptance by others as a platform for influence! That's great, and there's nothing wrong with this kind of influence, but this seminar taught that, although personality leadership is a type of leadership, it is not the best type.

I was getting more and more interested in this leadership training. I was a young Christian at the time and was relating it more to my Christian life than to my management position. What was the best type of leadership?

The seminar leader named a third type, *competence leadership*. Competence leadership is becoming a leader to others because you know how to do something that they don't know how to do. A good mechanic has competence leadership to me because of my little-or-no-knowledge of auto mechanics. A good speller is asked by others how to spell certain unusual words. A good mathematician is asked to calculate numbers for his friends. By our expertise in an area we become leaders, using that ability as a platform to influence others. But at this seminar the presenter went on to say that competence leadership, too, was not the best type of leadership.

So, position, personality and competence are all types of leadership, but not the best.

He finally described the best type of leadership. He called it *character* or *example leadership*. Now I was excited. Even the secular world was saying that character or example leadership is the best type of leadership. Every person can possess this kind of leadership. Every one of us can be a character leader at our school or on our job by doing what we're supposed to be doing, by being the right kind of role model. Being an upperclassman that just really seeks to do right influences other people. Being the right kind of employee or neighbor makes you a leader and makes you the best type of influence where God has placed you. Character leadership does provide salt and light. This was very significant to me as a young man and as one young in the Lord, because I Timothy 4:12 states, *Let no man despise thy youth; but be thou an example of the believers, in word, in conversation, in love, in spirit, in faith, in purity.* The Apostle Paul was urging young Timothy to develop the character qualities that would make him a leader by example. This meant to me that, even as a young Christian, I could be a quality leader by seeking to be obedient to God's Word.

But God uses all types of leadership, But the best leadership proceeds from character.
LEAD BY EXAMPLE!

Summary

- A difference noticed by others:

  - Christians have the privilege of being salt—seasoning, preserving, healing.

  - Christians have the privilege of being light—illuminating, penetrating, and revealing.

- Two key reminders:

  - In order to make a difference you have to be different.

  - You cannot change the quality of your surroundings by being more of the same.

- What is leadership?

  - Leadership is influence—the ability to influence someone in a direction that you think is important.

  - There are four types of leadership:

    1. Position
    2. Personality
    3. Confidence
    4. Example

For Consideration and Action

- Are you being salt in your home, church, workplace, school? How? What more could you do in this area?

- How have you been light in your home, church, workplace, school?

- Name a situation in which you became different by standing for what is right.

- Are you helping to change the quality of your situations?

- How are you helping to change the quality of some situation that needs changing?

- Name at least one change that you could make to be a biblical leader in your words, actions, spirit, love, faith, purity.

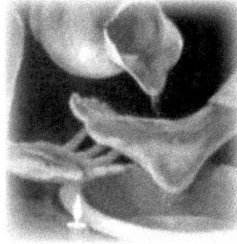

A DIFFERENT GOAL

by Matt Williams

Two years of Army service, including a tour of duty in Viet Nam, may have *saved* my life. In those two years, when my life was sometimes in jeopardy, and when I sometimes felt that my personal goals had been put on hold, someone else continued to pursue those same goals. What I found in his life when I returned saved me from wasting my own life. Let me explain.

Throughout the book of Romans, the word *therefore* signals major conclusions, the points toward which the Holy Spirit has been building as a lawyer builds a case. In the early chapters the word *therefore* is used three times to introduce the doctrine presented. In chapter 3: 20 *therefore* describes our complete inability to redeem ourselves: *Therefore by the deeds of the law there shall no flesh be justified in his sight.* In chapter 5:1 the word *therefore* refers to our being justified by faith: *Therefore being justified by faith, we have peace with God through our Lord*

Jesus Christ. In chapter 8:1 this word gives us our assurance in Christ: *There is therefore now no condemnation to them which are in Christ Jesus, who walk not after the flesh, but after the spirit.* In chapter 12:1-2 there is a fourth *therefore* which transitions from the extensive development of the case to the Holy Spirit's divine demand for a decision:

> *I beseech you therefore, brethren, by the mercies of God, that ye present your bodies a living sacrifice, holy, acceptable unto God, which is your reasonable service.*

> *And be not conformed to this world: but be ye transformed by the renewing of your mind, that ye may prove what is that good, and acceptable, and perfect will of God.*

This transitional verse presents the responsibility we have as believers because of what we have been given in Christ. Of the four characteristics of a Christian given in Romans 12:1-2, the first is our duty to *present* ourselves, as living sacrifices, back to God, who made us. Our goal is to become more like Christ, versus becoming more like the world. The process is described as *presenting our bodies…to God;* the analysis is that it is only *reasonable* to do so; and the result is that we *experience* the will of God for our lives and find that it is *good* for us, *acceptable* to us, and *perfectly* suited to the way God has made us. Therefore, any goal worth pursuing in life proceeds from this total availability to God.

Our Goal—To Become Like Christ

Romans 8:29 tells us this: that we are to take upon ourselves the copying of Christ. *For whom he did foreknow, he also did predestinate to be conformed to the image of his Son, that he might be the firstborn among many brethren.* We are to be conformed to Christ's image, to be like Him.

Even though we know we can never be just like Him in this life, what would it be like to seek earnestly to live like Jesus Christ daily? For one thing it would show up as wisdom in our daily lives. Wisdom is seeing the situations of life from God's viewpoint and handling them His way. Isaiah 43:1-7 tells us that we are here to glorify God. After saying, *"Fear not: for I have redeemed thee, I have called thee by thy name; thou art mine,"* and *"When thou passest through the waters, I will be with thee;"* and after reaffirming that we are precious in His sight, Jehovah God says, *"...Even every one that is called by my name: for I have created him for my glory."* Have you ever thought about that? That's really why we are here—to glorify God. This is another result of being conformed to the image of Christ. Do you realize that, if you really seek to glorify God with your life, you can influence others by what you do, and you can leave this earth one day in the future knowing that there are people that you have influenced for God?

The World's View of Success

The average person has the following as goals:

Popularity

In some sense, most people desire to be *popular*. People spend a lifetime seeking popularity and fame in their various forms. The desire of the average teen or adult is to be liked by those around him or her.

Power

The desire to take control is natural. It can manifest itself in a proud attitude, however well hidden, of being the one in charge. It may also be expressed in frustration at *not* being in control. Most people like being in charge, being the person calling the shots, telling others what to do. We all like getting our way, and this often comes with power.

Pleasure

This is the philosophy reflected in the "just have fun" attitude. This may be the person who says, "Hey, it's Friday, and that makes it a good day on the job." It can be the high school student whose first question at school is, "What can we do in class today to have fun?" There is nothing wrong with having fun, but we should not have this as our goal in life.

Have you ever gone into a convenience store in the late afternoon or early evening? You walk in to pay for your gasoline and see people on their way home from work. Like you, they are buying their gasoline, but they are also buying their 6-pack (or even 12-pack) of beer for the evening. They have worked hard all day. They feel that they deserve a "cold one" while they watch a ball game, and, if there's change left over, they buy a lottery ticket or two. We live in a society of "I just wanna have fun."

Possessions

That's the get-rich goal, the god of materialism, which always has been a glittering, hollow idol.

This is the goal that was so drastically changed by those two years when my life was put on hold by a tour of duty with the U.S. Army. I was a young man in the business world, trying to move up the corporate ladder. I had been working for the J.C. Penney Company for a few months, and I really wanted to be successful in sales and management. One night we weren't very busy in the store, and I took the absence of customers as my opportunity to talk with one of my superiors. I had been impressed with this successful manager. He seemed to be moving right up the ladder, and I had the same great visions for my future. I wanted to be a store manager and maybe even, someday, a district manager. I really wanted to move up in the J.C. Penney Company, as he was doing. So, I approached him, "Can

I ask you some questions? Tell me, how can I be successful?" First of all he pulled out his checkbook and showed me his balance. Then he began to share with me his philosophy. He said, "Aw, that's an easy one. You just give your life over to the J.C. Penney Company." I began taking mental notes. I had the thrilling sense of getting the inside scoop. He said, "Never take a day off." I noted, "Okay—never take a day off." He said, "If you take a day off, somebody might look better than you look that day, so you'd better never be gone from the store. Always make sure you are here, and you'll always look the best." I was impressed. He continued telling me all about the money he had made. He said he had recently purchased a brand new boat—he did mention that he hadn't had time to put it in the water yet—but he *had* this new boat. I thought, "Wow! That's what I want! Rich, and lots of toys!" I was ready to sell out to this philosophy.

However, it did not happen that way. A few months later I came home from work one night and there was a letter for me from someone named Sam, *Uncle* Sam. He said he wanted me for the next two years. So I saw my career come to a halt while I spent two years in the United States Army. One of those years was in Viet Nam. For the entire two years I wanted to get back to J.C. Penney and work my way to the top with the philosophy I had learned from that manager.

I found some interesting—and disturbing—developments when I got back home. In those two years he had moved up a little bit on the corporate ladder. However, during the time that I had been gone, his wife had divorced him. He lived by himself, and he seemed very lonely. Even then, before I became a Christian, I began to see that maybe there were some flaws in this philosophy that I had been adopting. Maybe there was another perspective about what's really important in life. My two years in the Army saved my life, not from death, but from the death-in-life of following empty goals that lead only to bitter disappointment.

If we are going to be biblical leaders, leaders by example, we need to understand the proper goals and priorities for a Christian. What are your goals today? Are they in line with God's goals? Isaiah 43:1-7 tells us that God has created us for His glory. Therefore, we are to take upon ourselves the copying of Jesus Christ. That has never been easy; it has always gone against our fallen nature. Yet, it is becoming ever increasingly difficult to live out that goal in contemporary society.

What Faces the Believer Today?

By new birth, we are strangers in this world system; by the granting of a heavenly citizenship, we have become expatriates in a society that is hostile to the heavenly land of our allegiance. John chapter 17 shares three vital principles for the Christian.

1. He has been redeemed out of the world—*I have manifested thy name unto the men which thou gavest me out of the world.* — 17:6.

    This is the *believer's purging*. We have been saved from the world. We do not need the world for satisfaction or happiness.

2. He is to live differently in the world—*And now I am no more in the world, but these are in the world, and I come to thee.*—17:11.

    This is the *believer's presence*. Matthew 5:16 adds the image of light: *Let your light so shine before men, that they may see your good works, and glorify your Father which is in heaven.* God wants us to be salt and light in a lost and dying world.

3. He is no longer in harmony with the world—*I have given them thy word; and the world hath hated them, because they are not of the world, even as I am not of the world. I pray not that thou shouldst take them out of the world, but that thou shouldst keep them from the evil. They are not of the world, even as I am not of the world.*—17:14-16

    This is the *believer's philosophy*. Jesus prayed not that God would take us out of the world, but that He would keep us from the evil of it, even as Christ was not of this world. Our philosophy is that we are in the world, but not a part of the world.

4. He is sent to the world—*As thou hast sent me into the world, even so have I also sent them into the world.* —17:18

    This is the *believers' purpose.* Just as the Heavenly Father sent Christ to earth on a mission, our mission and purpose is to influence those in the world around us.

The World Has an Aggressive Strategy

1. We live in a world of *opposing values.*

    Gods' goals are not the goals we see and hear around us. Every day we see and here the promotion of a philosophy that is contrary to God's standard. The world's philosophy tells us how to be successful, what to wear, where to go, what to be.

2. We live in a world of *aggressive strategies.* Our society attempts to tell us what our goals should be and how to be accepted by others. It is not a subtle approach. It is a blatant attempt to sell us on how to succeed in life.

3. We must either *adopt or reject* the world's values. There is no in-between. We are either adopting or rejecting the philosophy of the world around us. The very act of keeping silent is a capitulation to the world's demand to silence the disquieting voice of God.

4. In order to reject this world's philosophy, we must be *equally aggressive with God's plan.*

    This is our goal in this book—to help you become confident in living out God's plan for your life.

Let's be aggressive about giving our lives to God's will and to living out His plan. John 17:17 gives us the overview of this plan: *Sanctify them through thy truth: thy word is truth.* God's plan is for us to live by His Word, actively following His plan for victory and success. In doing this, we will be God's change agents wherever we are; this is leadership.

The *therefore* of Romans 12:1 refers to the goodness of God and the reasonableness of giving ourselves totally to His goals. If this world is aggressively opposed to God, we—as grateful children of God, redeemed, changed, and indwelt by the greatest power of the universe—should not be timid about declaring our direction and living up to our desire to make a difference for the One who has made all the difference for us.

"Therefore": AGGRESSIVELY LIVE OUT GOD'S PLAN!

Summary

- The Christian's goal in life: Christlikeness. (Romans 8:29, Isaiah 43:7)

- The world's view of success: fame, fortune, power, pleasure.

- God's view of success. (John 17)

  - The believer has been redeemed out of the world.
  - The believer is to live differently in the world.
  - The believer is no longer in harmony with the world.
  - The believer is sent to the world.

- The reality of, and response to, this world's system.

  - We live in a world of opposing values.
  - We live in a world of aggressive strategies.
  - We either adopt or reject the world's values.
  - In order to reject the world's philosophy, we must be equally aggressive with God's plan.

For Consideration and Action

- What are your primary goals as a believer?

  - How have your goals been shown to others through your actions in the past week?
  - Do you have a Christian worldview for living, as it is stated in John 17? Review this passage.
  - What can you do to aggressively live out God's plan this week?

Chapter 4

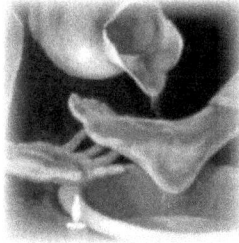

A DIFFERENT AUTHORITY: GOD'S WORD

by Ken Collier

My father was a wiz at finding golf balls! If anyone in our group lost a ball, Dad would walk right to the ball, no matter how far it strayed from the fairway. He often tried to impart his system to me, but with little success. He always said, "Son, mark the exact spot the ball goes into the woods by picking out a tree or bush; then walk directly to that spot!" It seemed simple enough, but to a twelve-year-old boy, there were just too many interesting things to look at and to think about between where I hit the ball and where it went into the woods. My Dad unconsciously marked the tree every time; therefore, I hatched a little plan. Since he could always find the ball, I would lag behind a few steps, and he would invariably lead me to the right spot. One day he asked me which tree I had marked, and the result is better left unpublished! Dad was the expert and worthy to be followed. He used an objective mark to get to the right place successfully. As my "golf ball finding" authority, he led me with confidence, and I followed him with confidence because he proved himself the expert over and over!

God's Word Must Be Our Authority

A godly servant-leader is different from others because he uses an authoritative, objective reference point, the Bible, whenever he learns or whenever he teaches others. He is different from secular counselors and psychologists; we take that for granted. Of course, he is different from friends or neighbors offering their advice and opinions over back fences, beside water coolers, and at school lunchroom tables. But we in our Bible-believing circles would do well to consider how much of our counsel, how many of our opinions, are really based on the Word of God. We sometimes get comfortable with saying "I think..." and "I feel . . ." without considering whether we could offer solid, Scriptural reasons for what we are saying. Allowing someone to follow me to a golf ball is one thing. Telling someone to follow me as I teach him to know and love God is quite another. Influencing others to love and serve God is a critical thing; therefore, the godly leader dare not stray from the objective standard that God has given for all of life and godliness:

> *According as his divine power hath given unto us all things that pertain unto life and godliness, through the knowledge of him that hath called us to glory and virtue: Whereby are given unto us exceeding great and precious promises: that by these ye might be partakers of the divine nature, having escaped the corruption that is in the world through lust. (II Peter 1:3-4)*

Note that what the *divine power* gives us is given *through the knowledge of Him that hath called us.* The more direct that knowledge of God is, the more powerful it is; and the direct source is the light of the Word of God. As examples, we have a responsibility to be clean reflectors of that light so that it is not clouded, colored, or distorted; but, even then, we should teach and explain, whenever appropriate, how our actions are based on the Bible.

Occasionally when traveling through Sanford, North Carolina, I go past a couple of roads named "Two-notch Road" and "Three-notch Road." It is easy to imagine the long-ago pioneer or farmer taking his trusty axe and chopping two or three notches into the tree at an out-of-the-way fork in the road. Then the farmer could say with authority, "Turn right when you come to the two notches." Of course, that marker would be there only as long as the tree was there. As leaders, we can never go wrong by leading with the permanent truth of God, rightly divided. In Isaiah 55:10-11 we read,

> For as the rain cometh down, and the snow from heaven, and returneth not thither, but watereth the earth, and maketh it bring forth and bud, that it may give seed to the sower, and bread to the eater: So shall my word be that goeth forth out of my mouth: it shall not return unto me void, but it shall accomplish that which I please, and it shall prosper in the thing whereto I sent it.

The markers God has established are permanent and trustworthy, and they are not going away.

A godly leader, whether he is a sixteen-year-old high school student, a twenty-six-year-old English teacher, a thirty-six-year-old father or a fifty-six-year-old pastor, possesses one thing that sets him apart from leaders in all other fields—he has a never-failing authority. He has access to the inspired, inerrant, and infallible Word of God. Allow several very familiar verses to impact you anew regarding the treasure of confidence that we possess as Christian leaders.

The grass withereth, the flower fadeth: but the word of our God shall stand for ever. (Isaiah 40:8)

All scripture is given by inspiration of God, and is profitable for doctrine, for reproof, for correction, for instruction in righteousness: That the man of God may be perfect, throughly furnished unto all good works. (II Timothy 3:16-17)

For the word of God is quick, and powerful, and sharper than any two-edged sword, piercing even to the dividing asunder of soul and spirit, and of the joints and marrow, and is a discerner of the thoughts and intents of the heart. (Hebrews 4:12)

For the word of the Lord is right; and all his works are done in truth. (Psalm 33:4)

...For thou hast magnified thy word above all thy name. (Psalm 138:2b)

Heaven and earth shall pass away, but my words shall not pass away. (Matthew 24:35)

Did you find yourself just skimming these Scriptures, just waiting to get to the next paragraph? To my shame, I do this too! But we must know the Word of God itself. We dare not let it, by familiarity, become merely an assumed backdrop. When we speak to people, advise people, or command someone, are we scrolling through Scripture in our minds asking the Holy Spirit to guide us to the correct portion of the living Word, just the right verses to meet this person's need? In our leadership we are apt to become good, proven, advice-giving leaders rather than good, objective, Word-giving leaders. We can, after much experience, forget to give the objective Word of God. Perhaps you should go back and read the foregoing list of verses once more, thoughtfully. Determine to direct others to God's Word!

How confident was Jesus Christ in the words and instructions He gave to the people among whom He worked and ministered? Of course, He was supremely confident. He was using His own Word, which, by itself, was powerful enough to bring the worlds into existence. Imagine, when Christ spoke of His Kingdom, there was no guesswork, because He had already been there. When He gave commands concerning marriage, He had no doubt about whether or not He got matters straight, because He invented marriage. When He spoke of creation, He was not guessing; He is the Creator. When He spoke of eternity, He knew: He was and is already there. No wonder people decided to forego eating for the privilege of hearing Him speak about life. He designed and created life. This was the *authority* speaking! People were amazed wherever He went because… *he taught them as one having authority, and not as the scribes.* (Matthew 7:29)

Staying in Touch with Reality

God's different kind of leader is determined not to stray from the Bible. I remember watching a flight attendant during a particularly turbulent flight make his way down the aisle. The plane was tossing and pitching, but he was walking briskly and confidently with a smile on his face. His confidence, I am sure, encouraged some of the nervous passengers. Watching carefully, I noticed the secret of his stability. He would use the back of his hand pushing against the seats to steady himself. He was not making an outward, laborious show of it. His hands were low, below the waist, but his tactic gave surety to his walk. He was never out of contact with a solidly secured seat as he confidently strolled the aisle. Even so, God's leader should never be out of contact with the commands and principles of Scripture as he walks or as he leads. His stability comes from being continually in touch with the wisdom found in the Word of His God. Since we have *the* authority, the secret is to never stray from it. Let your mind page through Scriptures you have studied and "touch" the nearest commandment—the one most clearly applying to the current need—as you deal with people today. Any other advice we could conjure up would be second best, and it may be just plain wrong. Being a godly leader means you must always "touch" the nearest command of God.

Do we want to be different on purpose? We must be careful to rightly use the right authority!

Keep "in touch" with real authority:
LIVE AND COUNSEL BY GOD'S WORD!

Summary

- God's Word must be our final authority in our choices and decisions.

    ○ Biblical leaders have access to the never-failing, inspired, inerrant, and infallible Word of God by which to lead with surety at all times.

- Isaiah 40:8—God's Word stands forever and is forever profitable.

    ○ Our advice should be aligned with the objective standard of God's Word, not simply what we "think" or "feel" is correct.

    ○ Reality comes as we continually touch the next commandment, thereby being in touch with the wisdom provided by God to each of His children.

For Consideration and Action

- For yourself

    ○ Have your decisions over the past week been based on God's Word or your own experiences of the past and opinions that you have?

    ○ Is there a Scripture from a chapter that you can memorize and mediate on this week that will help in making biblical decisions?

    ○ What's up? What choices and decisions do you have coming up this week?

- For your relationships to others

    ○ As a leader, are you aware of thinking and imparting Scripture in your giving of advice to friends, family, and fellow workers?

    ○ What can you do this week to test the advice and counsel you are giving to see if it is in line with God's Word?

What do you think could be the result of giving advice that may be well-intentioned, but not in accord with the words of the Bible?

Chapter 5

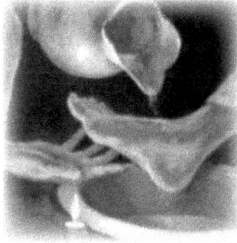

A DIFFERENT LEADERSHIP

by Matt Williams

Biblical leadership begins with the *giving* of our *wills back to God*. This will bring a different attitude to our lives—one of following Christ and putting Him first. If we live this way, it will show in our relationships with others, and it will be the foundation for all true leadership. Let's take a look at two opposing kinds of leadership.

Ruler Leadership: The World's View

Worldly Leadership: The Primer Course

As I think about leadership, I consider my days in high school to be a microcosm of the typical leadership seen at any level, whether adult or teen; whether in society, government, or business, or, all too often, in the church. I attended a private school. It was not a Christian school, but it was a religious school. I found plenty of student leadership there, but it was not biblical leadership.

I came to this school from another city and knew very few people. That made freshman initiation all the more memorable—for all the wrong reasons! On this day the seniors did all that they could to make the freshmen feel as low as possible. Freshmen had to do anything that the seniors told them to do. If a senior wanted his victim to stand on the lab table in chemistry and sing a song how much the freshman loved him, the freshman had to do it because that was part of the initiation. The only thing I can remember about freshman initiation is that I was thinking, "Man, I cannot wait! Four years from now I will be a senior." I was waiting for the day that I got to do to others what they were doing to me. I was learning a style of leadership from the upperclassmen. Eventually these freshmen would become seniors, and then they would call the shots; they would be the ones that pretty much ran everything. Then, at the end of the school year, they would graduate and move on.

That leads us, however, to the last lesson in this primer course on worldly leadership. In the fall many of last year's seniors would go off to college, but some of those that didn't would come back to visit the high school, normally in mid-to-late October. It was as if they were thinking, "I want to go back where I'm a 'somebody.' " They would walk onto the campus hoping to impress everybody as they did the year before. But the interesting thing about it was that, as they walked around the campus, the new seniors would look at them as if to say, "Who are you? You had your day last year, and now it's my turn. I'm the senior; I'm the one in charge now. What are you doing coming back? This is our turf; this is our territory now." And really, they didn't seem to fit in anymore. That was my introduction to the world's view of leadership.

There are two opposing views of leadership. The typical world-style leader is the "ruler leader": *one who dominates and usually gets his way, but leaves behind little or nothing of value and is rarely missed when he is gone.* It is just like those seniors who would come back to the old campus, as if to say, "Hey, here I am, last year's senior." We weren't impressed anymore because they had their day. They had dominated long enough, and now it was someone else's turn. Many Christians are functioning the same way: "I am going to use *my position*, I am going to use *my power*, I am going to use *my popularity*, and I am going to use that *to get what I want*." I saw the ruler leadership concept continue when I entered the business world. The idea was to "win them over" for my sale, for my gain, for my personal fame.

What's in It for Me?

This is a common approach to life: What's in it for me? I observed a classic example of this on a soccer field a couple of years ago. A certain player was getting frustrated and angry. His team was losing the game, and he was yelling at the top of his lungs, "Pass me the ball! I want to score!" The ruler leader's motivation behind these demands translates this way: "Make me look good. I want to be the hero." And it's not just teens at school. There are ruler leaders everywhere in government, in industry, in management, and even in ministry. People naturally are self-centered, wanting all the attention focused on themselves.

But what is God's plan? What does God expect of a student who is a junior, a senior, sophomore, or a freshman in a Christian school? What is God's plan for a parent? Or a teacher? Or an employer? What is God's plan for us? To have God's strategy, we must reject man's plan and adopt God's plan for biblical leadership.

Biblical Leadership—Christ's View

Three Survival Principles

We have already seen that our responsibility according to Mark 10:42-45 is to be ministers. Let's think about your job or your school. Who are the people that are "the greatest"? Is it those who have the positions and titles and power? Consider your home. Does the hierarchy go from the top, the one who tells others what to do, to the bottom, the one who gets stuck with the jobs no one wants to do? *But so shall it not be among you: but whosoever will be great among you shall be your [servant].* (Mark 10:43) Is this the kind of leadership that we bring to our world? Leadership is not how many serve you, but how many you serve. It's being excited about seeing the Master successful in the lives of other people. And with each position of leadership comes a greater responsibility to serve those under our authority. This makes our influence a great training ground for future servant-leaders.

Let's examine the three key principles that make biblical leadership the avenue of God's power.

Principle #1—*Be a minister*

But Jesus called them to him, and saith unto them, Ye know that they which are accounted to rule over the Gentiles exercise lordship over them; and their great ones exercise authority upon them. But so shall it not be among you: but whosoever will be great among you, shall be your minister: And whosoever of you will be the chiefest, shall be servant of all. For even the Son of man came not to be ministered unto, but to minister, and to give his life a ransom for many. (Mark 10:42-45)

Servant of all! When I think of this principle, my thoughts go to a situation that took place a few years ago. When I first traveled to Mexico, I attended a pastors' conference in a little village called Chouchacoyo. Pastors had traveled from all around this mountainous region to attend. Some came by car, some by truck, some even walked or rode mules or horses to attend. It was a wonderful conference, and those of us from our church had a great time. One of our most notable experiences was the sleeping situation. It was simple: just find a spot, put your bedroll down, and enjoy a good night's rest. We did. In fact, we found some old army-style fold-up beds behind the church. We set them up outside and slept under the stars. It was great!

The following year I was able to attend the conference again, this time as a speaker. I brought five other men from our church with me. When we arrived, I told them about the army beds, and we went to look for them. They were not to be found. Soon it was time for the service to begin. Following the service, my friends and I were outside fellowshipping with the people. A man approached and, through a translator, asked me if I wanted a bed. "Ah!" I thought, "This man must know where the army beds are." So I replied, "Yes." He left, and we continued to fellowship. About 45 minutes later I saw a man climbing that steep dirt road toward the church. He had a large object strapped to his back—a piece of foam and a wooden frame. This man had gone home and gotten his bed from his home, the bed that he and his wife slept on, and he was bringing it for me. "I didn't mean for him to bring his bed. I can't take his bed!" I said to the translator. "No, he wants you to have it. He would be hurt if you didn't accept his service," was the reply. This man understood the principle of being a minister. He didn't have much, but he used what he had to minister. What can we do today to serve someone else? We have gifts, talents, abilities, and possessions. God wants us to use what we have to be a blessing to others. Biblical leadership is taking what we have and giving it back to God by ministering to others.

Life Principle—Walk slowly through the crowd, Matthew 9:36.

As we go about our daily responsibilities, be conscious of the needs of those around us. See the needs, sense the needs, survey the needs by asking questions. "...When Jesus saw the multitudes He was moved with compassion."

Principle #2—*Have the mind of Christ*

Let nothing be done through strife or vainglory, but in lowliness of mind let each esteem other better than themselves. Look not every man on his own things, but every man also on the things of others. Let this mind be in you, which was also in Christ Jesus: Who, being in the form of God, thought it not robbery to be equal with God: But made himself of no reputation, and took upon him the form of a servant, and was made in the likeness of men: And, being found in fashion as a man, he humbled himself and became obedient unto death, even the death of the cross. Wherefore, God also hath highly exalted him, and given him a name which is above every name, That at the name of Jesus every knee should bow, of things in heaven, and things in earth, and things under the earth, And that every tongue should confess that Jesus Christ is Lord to the glory of God, the Father. (Philippians 2:3-11)

This passage presents four key thoughts:

1. Put *others* before *yourself,* v. 3.

2. Have the *mind* of *Christ in all that you do,* v. 5.

3. Christ made *Himself* of *no reputation,* v. 7.

4. Christ *became obedient* unto *death,* v. 8.

These practices—illustrated through the life of Jesus Christ—sum up biblical leadership. This is having the mind of Christ. The one underlying foundation of all is not to think of ourselves and what is best for us. Like Christ, we must choose to make ourselves of no reputation and to become obedient to the will of our Heavenly Father, having as our one desire to see the Master successful in the lives of those around us.

Last summer I had the privilege of heading up a mission trip to Mexico with over eighty adults and teens from our church. Our theme for the week was Philippians 2:5, having the mind of Christ. What a week we had! Even before we got into Mexico, the Christlike attitudes and actions manifested by members of the mission team greatly impacted each other's lives as well as the lives of others outside our group. It was an unbelievable week, one we will never forget, a week which glorified God to both Christians and non-believers in Mexico. As I heard testimonies of Christian teens and adults seeking to have the mind of Christ, it occurred to me to wonder, "Do we have to travel hundreds of miles to a foreign country to display the mind of Christ?" No. We can focus on Philippians 2 and these vital principles every day if we choose.

Life Principle—Let your purpose prioritize your life, Romans 12:2.

As mentioned before, Romans 12 gives all believers the ultimate purpose for life—"Be ye transformed by the renewing of your mind, that ye may prove...."

Principle #3—*Wash dirty feet*

Now before the feast of the passover, when Jesus knew that his hour was come that he should depart out of this world unto the Father, having loved his own which were in the world, he loved them unto the end. And supper being ended, the devil having now put into the heart of Judas Iscariot, Simon's son, to betray him; Jesus knowing that the Father had given all things unto his hands, and that he was come from God, and went to God; He riseth from supper and laid aside his garments; and took a towel, and girded himself. After that he poureth water into a basin, and began to wash the disciples' feet, and to wipe them with the towel wherewith he was girded.

So after he had washed their feet, and had taken his garments, and was set down again, he said unto them, Know ye what I have done to you? Ye call me Master and Lord: and ye say well; for so I am. If I then, your Lord and Master, have washed your feet; ye also ought to wash one another's feet. For I have given you an example, that ye should do as I have done to you. Verily, verily I say unto you, The servant is not greater than his lord; neither he that is sent greater than he that sent him. If you know these things, happy are ye if ye do them. (John 13:1-5, 12-17)

Let's think about this passage and the role that Jesus Christ played here. This is not really about removing dust. Attitudes, not actions, are the heart of this being a servant of all. If the attitude is right, the actions will be there. We are talking about someone who doesn't just *do servant things,* but someone who *is a servant.*

We use the term *servant* commonly around our churches, and I'm afraid that sometimes we get the idea that being a servant is based on what we *do.* I may think I'm a servant if I have a good voice and I sing solos at church. I serve by singing a solo. Or, I'm an usher and serve the Lord by ushering. Or I'm a cheerleader; I try to get a lot of spirit going in our school, and I serve by doing that. Or I'm an officer in my class, and I try to help my class. Those things are all good; there is nothing wrong with any of those things. It's great to be involved, and the Lord can use those activities. However, I'm afraid that we sometimes think that if we are doing those things, then we are servants. No. A servant doesn't just do servant things, but as he does those things, he serves. The difference is primarily in our motives. So what is the objective of being on a team? Is it helping everyone else? What is the objective of being an usher? Is it helping people feel comfortable as they come to church so that they are not distracted from the message?

Life Principle—Be different on purpose, Matthew 5:16.

Let your purpose prioritize your life—and this purpose is to "let your light so shine before men, that they may see your good works, and glorify your Father which is in Heaven."

Don't just do little servant things,
BE A SERVANT!

Summary
- There are two views of leadership:
    - ° Ruler leadership (Mark 10:42)
    - ° Biblical leadership (Mark 10:43-45)

- Ruler leadership defined—dominating and usually getting one's own way, but leaving nothing or very little of value behind.

- Biblical leadership defined—serving God while serving people, and being excited about seeing the Master successful in their lives.

- There are three principles for being a biblical leader:
    - ° Be a minister, that is, a servant. (Mark 10:42-45)
    - ° Have the mind of Christ. (Philippians 2:3-5)
    - ° Wash dirty feet. (John 13:3-5, 12-17)

For Consideration and Action
- Much of what we do is a product of our experiences or opinions. Look back on your leadership this past week. Have you been a ruler leader or biblical leader?

- What are some ways in which you can see the Master successful in the lives of those around you?

- Think on the principle of "walk slowly through the crowd." (Matthew 9:36) How can you implement that in your life?

- Think on the life principle "let your purpose prioritize your life." (Romans 12:1-2) How can you put that into practice this week?

- Think on the life principle of "being different on purpose." (Matthew 5:16) How can you put that into practice in your actions and attitudes this week?

Chapter 6

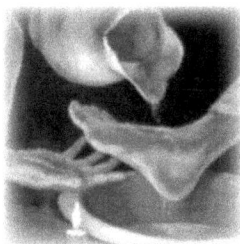

A DIFFERENT SPIRIT

by Matt Williams

W e are ready to move to the empowering element behind all that we have seen thus far. Behind the differences in leadership style, authority, or goals is an absolute essential. Without this factor, the heart is not really different, and without this we have missed the message of Christ, our example. Come with me and view one of the most tender moments in the life of Christ on earth, a moment that defines servant leadership.

> *Now before the feast of the passover, when Jesus knew that his hour was come that he should depart out of this world unto the Father, having loved his own which were in the world, he loved them unto the end. And supper being ended, the devil having now put into the heart of Judas Iscariot, Simon's son, to betray him; Jesus knowing that the Father had given all things into his hands, and that he was come from God, and went to God; He riseth from supper, and laid*

aside his garments; and took a towel, and girded himself. After that he pioureth water into a bason, and began to wash the disciples' feet, and to wipe them with the towel wherewith he was girded. (John 13:1-5)

We looked at the principle of leadership from this passage in the last chapter. But it also shares much about the spirit of Jesus Christ. There are four principles in this passage that show us what it was in the life of the Lord Jesus Christ that made Him the most influential leader of all time. Three of these are elements that we must allow God to develop supernaturally in us. The fourth is a joyful by-product of living God's way.

We Must Have a Submissive Spirit

First, we see that Jesus Christ had a *submissive spirit.* Notice the deliberate contrast between His lofty position and His lowly service: *Jesus knowing that the Father had given all things unto him and that he was come from God and went to God, he riseth from supper and he laid aside his garments and he took a towel and he girded himself.* Then He washed the disciples' feet.

At this time it was a very common custom to wash the feet of guests as they came into a house. The guests had been wearing sandals, and their feet would naturally be covered with the dust of the road. A hired servant would greet them at the door with a basin and a towel, and would wash their feet as people entered the house. That was a servant's job, a lowly job. If that household didn't have a hired servant, one of two things would happen. Either the host or hostess of the house washed people's feet as they were coming in, or they would provide a basin and a towel at the door so people could wash their own feet.

John 13 does not give any of the details, but it is interesting to me that evidently no one had washed Jesus' feet. Perhaps the disciples were too busy in the preparation of the Passover meal. Maybe their focus was on who was going to get the position of honor, sitting closest to Jesus. However it happened, nobody thought of washing Christ's feet. They didn't even think of washing their own feet. Perhaps none of them wanted to jeopardize his image at a time when, as Mark 9 reveals, each was trying to gain recognition as the greatest. No one then wanted to assume the lowly position of a servant. Not much has changed, has it?

Therefore, the greatest of them all, Jesus Christ, the One whom they had been following for the last three years, the One whom they had seen do all the miracles, He was the one that submitted Himself to them and washed their feet. He had a submissive spirit. If we are going to be biblical leaders, it all begins with submission.

Ephesians 6:1-2 has always been a great challenge to children: *Children obey your parents in the Lord, for this is right.* It all begins with the outward action of obedience. And God blesses this submission,...*for this is right.* But it doesn't stop there: *Honor thy father and mother; which is the first commandment with promise.* It continues with the attitude of honoring parents. What can I do to make them succeed as parents? With the command comes a promise in verse 3, *that it may be well with thee, and thou mayest live long on the earth.* God promises a good life, a happy life, as children understand and practice this principle of submission. Jesus practiced this principle. After explaining to his parents that he "must be about my Father's business," (Luke 2:49) He practiced submission in verses 51 and 52: *And he went down with them, and came to Nazareth, and was subject unto them.* The product of submission comes in verse 52: *And Jesus increased in wisdom, and stature, and in favour with God and man.* This happened in the "silent years." It is the only recorded event between His very early years and the start of his public ministry. Christ's life shows the importance and impact of submission. And it doesn't stop with children and teens understanding and practicing it. Adults must continue to have the submissive spirit modeled in John 13. God will continue to bless a submissive spirit. He gave this example to his disciples for their practice.

We Must Have a Sensitive Spirit

The second thing that stands out in this passage is that Christ had a *sensitive spirit*, something like a spiritual antenna for the needs of other people. Jesus, *having loved his own which were in the world....* His focus was on these people in His care. Because He loved them, he was focused on their needs.

That sensitive spirit is absolutely essential for ministry. Are you known as one who has an antenna for the needs of other people? Can you detect when other people are hurting, and then do you try to be a help? We get so wrapped up in ourselves and our priorities and our needs that we forget to "look on the things of others" (Philippians 2: 4). Yet, leadership requires seeing and meeting the needs of others. We are familiar with the parable of the Good Samaritan (Luke 10:30-37). Others, even the religious leaders, passed by and even looked the other way. But the Samaritan was attentive to the needs, available to meet the needs, and active in taking total care of the needs of the stranger. In order to have a sensitive spirit, we must be attentive to the needs around us, ready and available to meet these needs, and quick to act in meeting these needs.

We Must Have a Sacrificial Spirit

Jesus' love that led to this service was not a short-term commitment; it was not a matter of convenience: *he loved them unto the end* (13:1). He showed a *true sacrificial spirit*. Genuine love is sacrificing yourself for the success of someone else. Jesus concluded this object lesson with,

For I have given you an example that ye should do as I have done to you (13: 15). When is the last time that you sacrificed for others? Do you seek to allow others to succeed by sacrificing some of yourself for their benefit? Even in the last hours before His death, His commitment was to benefit others. What a challenge for our service and ministry!

We Will Have a Satisfied Spirit

After three highly unorthodox expressions of leadership, Jesus gives the remarkable result. It is remarkable in that, after the world has failed to find this quality in all of its self-exalting, self-serving domination, this quality is found as a by-product of this forgotten form of leadership. The Lord Jesus declared in verse 17 that one who practices this servant-leadership will have a *satisfied spirit*. It says, *If you know these things, happy are ye if ye do them.*

The typical leader of this world looks enviously up whatever ladder he is climbing, and suspiciously down. He is very much concerned that he get the credit for what goes right and that someone else get the blame for what goes wrong. His attitude is contagious among those around him, producing a crowd of competitors for whatever he is trying to get, and the one thing he is most likely to get is ulcers! Would you like to be satisfied in your service? Be a biblical leader. Lead with submission, sincerity, and sacrifice, and you will have a satisfied spirit.

The boy who could not play baseball

A few years ago my oldest son, Kevin, was getting ready to graduate from high school. He already had a busy schedule for that spring, with graduation preparations on top of all the usual church and school activities of that time of year. He had planned a busy summer, too. One day at church, however, a staff member asked me if Kevin would be interested in coaching a little league team of seven and eight-year-olds for our ministry's baseball program. I said that his schedule was pretty busy, but that it would be all right to ask him. At home that night Kevin mentioned the situation and, after discussion, we decided that if he could get his friend Andy to help, they could probably handle the coaching.

I remember Kevin coming home after the first practice. "How did it go son?" I asked.

"Pretty good dad," was his reply. "I think we have a pretty good team." But then he mentioned one boy on the team. He couldn't throw the ball, couldn't catch, and couldn't hit. He was bad. And not only that, but the other boys were laughing at him.

I really did not expect to know the boy, because the little league is an outreach ministry of the church, and there are many boys involved from families I would not yet know, but I asked the boy's name. When Kevin told me, it sounded familiar. I asked him to describe the boy, and I thought I recognized him. "Son, he's from a single-parent home. This boy hasn't had a dad to teach him how to throw and catch. You will have a great opportunity to help this summer."

As the season progressed, they did have a good team. In fact, they won the championship. And Kevin and Andy had a great opportunity to help this little boy. No crowds roared approval as they taught a little boy how to throw a baseball, but they showed the love of Christ to a family with a need. It was lowly service, with few to notice, but among those few was the God of the universe. They were able to wash dirty feet that summer, and they found great joy and fulfillment in serving.

What about you? Is there someone you can help, someone whose needs you can meet? It takes that submissive spirit, that sensitive spirit, that sacrificial spirit. But, as you wash dirty feet, you will have a satisfied spirit.

Be great:
WASH DIRTY FEET!

Summary

- As we view the life of Christ we see four characteristics of a different type of spirit:

    ○ He demonstrated a submissive spirit—He submitted to all.

    ○ He demonstrated a sensitive spirit—He had a "spiritual antenna" to the needs of others.

    ○ He demonstrated a sacrificial spirit—He loved people "unto the end" and showed them through his actions.

    ○ He demonstrated a satisfied spirit—There is joy in serving. (John 13:17)

For Consideration and Action

- Are you submissive to God and the authorities in your life?

- Do you expect more honor from those under your authority than you give to those in authority over you?

- Do you have a sensitive spirit; having a "spiritual antenna" for the needs of other people? Name a way you displayed that in the past month.

- Do you consistently show a sacrificial spirit with your attitudes and actions?

- Are you satisfied? Is your Christian life truly the superior way of life?

Chapter 7

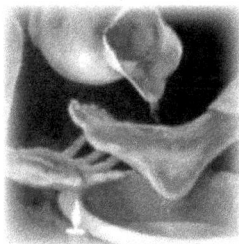

A DIFFERENT LOVE

by Ken Collier

I look forward to the discussion of this aspect of the servant-leader's life for a special reason. The study of godly love changed my wife's life and my life individually, and it changed our lives together. I believe it has had a great impact on our children also. I praise God for love that is not just natural and nice, but is also supernatural. The Bible says, *Love never faileth* (I Corinthians 13:8a). What an amazing statement! Is there anyone or anything that you know about which it could be said, "This product or this person will never fail"? Even the things we own that boast of a "lifetime guarantee" will fail. The lifetime guarantee simply means we can get another one just like it and that one will someday fail. Anything that never fails cannot be natural; it has to be beyond natural. And that is exactly what God's love is!

In the midst of our busiest years of child-raising and ministry growth, God brought my parents to live with us at The WILDS. Mom was succumbing to Alzheimer's disease, and Dad had cancer in addition to his severe heart condition. Dad was almost inconsolable at the gradual loss of Mom's reasoning. He became bitter, and this bitterness came out daily. The combination of children, parents, disease, and anger created a very full platter for us. Most of this stress fell on my wife, Mardi, as I had to continue the responsibilities of the ministry. At the point of breaking, we went back to the basics. We went back to love as it is found in I Corinthians 13. We began practicing this love in our dark times with an intensity that we may not have had in the easier times. We even told my dad what we were doing. The results, barely perceptible at first, soon became very obvious. We became a top-notch team, working together. Soon dad, who was already a Christian, changed dramatically! It was almost like a new, new birth! It was supernatural!

There is nothing new in what I have said. Yet, this example of God's power at work in daily life can be an encouragement to you as you desire to be that different kind of parent or child or pastor or deacon or teacher or employer or leader of any kind. Here is the type of love you must have if you are to leave the handprints of God on whatever task you handle, the mark which indicates that your work is not of earth, but is heavenly.

This Love Comes from God Alone

What can be more elementary: supernatural love cannot come from natural man. From the beginning God possessed a supernatural love that was amazing in that it did not change, even when its object was unworthy. It came from the heart of God. At our salvation we became the dwelling place of the God who is love (I John 4). Therefore, this amazing love dwells in us. When we practice this supernatural love, it will accomplish God's purpose. The results will always return to glorify God. It never fails.

Herein is love, not that we loved God, but that he loved us, and sent his Son to be the propitiation for our sins (I John 4:10).

And we have known and believed the love that God hath to us. God is love; and he that dwelleth in love dwelleth in God, and God in him (I John 4:16).

We love him, because he first loved us (I John 4:19).

The Lord hath appeared of old unto me, saying, Yea, I have loved thee with an everlasting love: therefore with lovingkindness have I drawn thee (Jeremiah 31:3).

Love Is Not an Option; It Is a Command

Biblical love is often associated with action verbs, as in these verses above: *he loved us, and sent his son,* and *with lovingkindness have I drawn thee.* If love were all emotion, it would seem strange that God should command people to *practice* it. However, godly love is not just a feeling; it produces visible results. Of course, our emotions are involved, but God has made it very plain to us that His love works through the trusting obedience of His children—regardless of how they feel at the time. We cannot just wait until we feel loving. We must act in love. We obey; He meets our willing, trusting hearts with His grace (a supernatural desire to do the right thing), and our lives and the lives of those we minister to are supernaturally changed! We are commanded to love God, our neighbors, our brothers and sisters in Christ, and even our enemies! It is a liberating truth to know that you do not have to feel loving in order to obey God's command to love. God gives the ability to love the unlovely. A godly leader should be known for godly love.

Here are the fast facts of God's command:

God *does* command us to love.

Then one of them, which was a lawyer, asked him a question, tempting him, and saying, Master, which is the great commandment in the law? Jesus said unto him, Thou shalt love the Lord thy God with all thy heart, and with all thy soul, and with all thy mind. This is the first and great commandment. And the second is like unto it, Thou shalt love thy neighbor as thyself. On these two commandments hang all the law and the prophets (Matthew 22:35-40).

God gives the ability to love.

Beloved, if God so loved us, we ought also to love one another. No man hath seen God at any time. If we love one another, God dwelleth in us, and his love is perfected in us (I John 4:11-12).

This love will be a noticeable mark of the Christian.

By this shall all men know that ye are my disciples, if ye have love one to another (John 13:35).

This love will be unexpected by the world's standards.

But I say unto you which hear, Love your enemies, do good to them which hate you, Bless them that curse you, and pray for them which despitefully use you (Luke 6:27-28).

Love Is Sacrificial; Not Self-Focused

The love given to us by God is sacrificial. Love is always the sacrificing of self for the benefit of another. The love of God led Him to the cross of Calvary. We should expect nothing less than the fact that love will require great sacrifice. It may not always lead to physical death, but it may lead to things that are just like dying to us. Often the question to ask is, "What is the thing that would be most like dying to me right now?"

Suppose you come home from a very difficult day of work, a day filled with people problems, and find your home filled with tension. It is obvious that something unpleasant has just happened. What do you do next? If you do the right thing, it will probably require a sacrifice of spiritual, emotional, and physical energy. It will cost you time. You will do the thing that is "most like dying" at that moment. The loving way is not always the unpleasant way, but many times the eagerness to sacrifice for the benefit of another is a key part of the solution. What is necessary at church, work, and school? The loving thing is often the thing that you would least like to do. It is the sacrificial thing. It is the thing that is most like dying.

Can you see the essential intertwining of love and sacrifice in these verses:

> *And he said to them all, If any man will come after me, let him deny himself, and take up his cross daily, and follow me* (Luke 9:23).

> *But God commendeth his love toward us, in that, while we were yet sinners, Christ died for us* (Romans 5:8).

> *For God so loved the world, that he gave his only begotten Son, that whosoever believeth in him should not perish, but have everlasting life* (John 3:16).

> *He that spared not his own Son, but delivered him up for us all, how shall he not with him also freely give us all things?* (Romans 8:32)

This is a universal truth of God's word: *love sacrifices*. But this universal truth is not only the key to the power of biblical leadership, but also the only path to enjoying the rewards of biblical love.

Love Is Practical

I Corinthians 13 shows us what the love of God practiced by our Lord Jesus Christ actually looks like. In this chapter we are specifically told what love *does* and *does not* do. It could hardly be made more practical. That's not to say it is easy. This is why servant-leadership excels: it can only be accomplished by God's grace. The following is a brief description of the characteristics of love as taken from this, the "Love Chapter."

Love suffereth long

Love is "long-tempered" and "long-fused" and practices patience with people. God will give me the ability to go beyond the normal point when I would fail. Being longsuffering means that I will concentrate on giving *(you insert the name of someone)* God's words and God's message in God's time, rather than giving him my words and my message in my time. When I am impatient, I am concentrating on my own self and what I want to say. When I am patient, I am concentrating on God and what He would like me to say to *(name of person)*. Being long suffering, I do not take *(name of person)* into my own hands. I give him back to God, for He owns him and knows what He wishes to accomplish in him. I am not the limit-setter or boundary-maker. God is. This being true, I need to practice the love of God by giving *(name of person)* only God's message and God's words in God's timing.

Love is kind

Love is eager to sacrifice itself for the benefit of another. Therefore, love is always active and useful to *(name of person)*. Kindness chooses the thing that will bring the most benefit and encouragement to him. In order to be kind to *(name of person)*, I will concentrate on giving him kind words, kind tones, my time, and some small gift that is sacrificial. Kindness is saying to *(name of person)*, "I think of you." I am selfish when I am being useful only to myself. I will be useful and active in *(name of person)'s* life, showing him the kindness that God has shown to me!

Love envieth not

Love doesn't boil or brood or stew over the success of another person, as if somehow someone else's success works against me. I cannot be envious of *(name of person)*, because his success cannot work against my success in God's plan. I must not be happy when he is sad; I must not be sad when he is happy. When I envy him, I am thinking in a totally unloving manner which demonstrates my lack of love toward God as well as toward *(name of person)*. The secret of not envying is to recognize that I have been given so much more than I deserve right now. It is to recognize that the thing which I most deserve, hell, I will never experience because of the grace and mercy of God. I cannot be so unloving and so ungrateful as to be envious of *(name of person)*.

Love vaunteth not itself, is not puffed up

Love is not a windbag. It doesn't parade itself around to attract attention. A person who loves God will not be impressed with himself. Since it is true that I tend to brag about whoever is first in my thoughts, help me not to think about impressing anyone with myself, but help me always to build the conversation around what my God means to me. I should never speak or act for the purpose of *(name of person)'s* being impressed with me. May I love God in such a way that *(name of person)* will be impressed with Christ alone. If I have the opportunity to steer the conversation, may it be steered to Christ; not to me!

Love doth not behave itself unseemly

Love acts like a gentleman or a lady; therefore, it does not present the love of God in an ugly, misshapen way. I must remember that when I am around *(name of person)*, I cannot be loud, overbearing, or crude. I cannot make fun of others, tease, gossip, or talk about others for my own pleasure, because these actions demonstrate a life that draws attention to myself and away from God. I must remember manners (*please, thank you, let me help, excuse me*). I should never be guilty of grossing people out and offending their sensibilities of right and proper things. May I be a gentleman or lady around (*name of person*) for Christ's sake.

Love seeketh not her own

Love doesn't insist on its own way. It doesn't inquire after and keep track of its own rights, time, money, hobbies, or free time to use in selfish pursuits; but it keeps track for the sole purpose of giving to God and others. Love is not a "Scrooge" or a miser. Love doesn't hoard what it possesses. It possesses in order to minister God's unexpected, surprising grace. This being true, am I continually not hoarding, but giving my resources as an example of the grace of God to (*name of person*)?

Love is not easily provoked

Love doesn't explode when it doesn't get its way. Being provoked means having my spirit "split apart." This is nothing but unrighteous anger! Do I get angry when my rights are ignored or not considered? As a Christian, all that I have has been given to me by God. I have no rights, since all I have has come from my Father and should be yielded back to Him. Do I still get angry with (*name of person*) for selfish causes? If I do not seek my own way, I won't become easily provoked with (*name of person*), thinking that he has taken what I deserve. Selfish anger demonstrates a lack of love toward God and (*name of person*).

Love thinketh no evil

Love doesn't make up excuses for evil. It doesn't keep a record of wrongs done against it for the purpose of bringing them back up at a later time. Do I hold any resentment against (*name of person*)? It is God's will that wrongs not be written down, but that they be handled and laid to rest permanently in the way God prescribes. I am not allowed to attempt to read (*name of person*)'s motives. To do so is unloving. I cannot know for certainty why he says what he says, nor why he does what he does. If I have resentment toward *(name of person)*, I must handle it right away with no delay. If I sense there is resentment from *(name of person)* toward me, I must go to him privately. I cannot hide evil in my thoughts toward *(name of person)*.

Love rejoiceth not in iniquity, but rejoiceth in the truth

Love gets no joy in that which is against the character of God. I can get no thrill enjoying anything for which Christ had to die on the Cross. I do not love God as I ought if I get joy out of any television program, Internet site, or production which has as its theme something that God condemns. I am not loving toward *(name of person)* if I am not careful of what I laugh at or enjoy. I cannot get joy out of iniquity.

Love rejoices in the truth

Love "joys together" with that which is true. True love loves what God loves as well as hates what God hates. By my example do I teach *(name of person)* to rejoice in that which God says is true? Does *(name of person)* "catch me" being devoted to God in my habits and my actions? Since all reality and truth are founded in God's principles, I must get my joy out of God's truth all day long.

Love beareth all things

Love covers all it can righteously cover. It doesn't ignore sin; it simply refers it back to the ones who can solve the problem. Those are always God, the offender, and the one who has been offended. While a sin problem is being handled, I must love *(name of person)* by covering him, protecting him from ridicule, exposure, and harm as much as I appropriately can. Am I guilty of talking about *(name of person)*'s sin to people who are not part of the problem or are part of the solution to the problem? I need to cover *(name of person)*'s sin, not broadcast it.

That is the loving thing to do.

Love believeth all things

Love believes the best about another person. It puts the best interpretation on an event and believes in the best outcome. Love does not rush to judgment of others without evidence. How quickly I believe evil about someone is an indicator about whether or not I have a godly love for him. This being true, I will choose to believe the best about *(name of person)*.

Love hopeth all things

Love does not talk and think about another person as if he were hopeless. Love takes on the problems of others and doesn't give up on them. Love always works hard toward the best outcome, believing that failure is not final. Love makes a person who appears to be hopeless or in a hopeless situation a serious matter of prayer and effort. I will have hope for *(name of person)*, and I will be steady under pressure. Love stays put when the "bullets are flying." Love never gives up on another person and will never let people go quietly into sin. This being true, I must persevere in my love for *(name of person)*, always hoping, never giving up!

This is truly a different kind of love. It is a love that transcends man's reason and ability. It is a different kind of love, and it is the calling card of the godly leader who would seek to be used in a supernatural way in the lives of others! The Holy Spirit of God takes the servant-leader's trusting obedience to do the loving thing at all times and uses it to make a difference in the lives of others. Godly love makes the difference and is powerful in action.

Begin the challenge of practicing God's supernatural love right away. There is someone with whom you have contact every day or almost every day. That person is not easy to love, and, frankly, his personality is such that you have had a hard time even pretending to love him. Now that you have your "victim" in mind, it is time to cry out to God to give you grace to love that one! You are not going to give him what he deserves; you are going to give him what God gave you. Any time spent personalizing and practicing this love is well spent. Whenever you go through the I Corinthians 13 list of qualities, have a person in mind. The person could be at home, at school, at work, at church, or in the non-Christian community. You are going to lay siege to his heart in godly love. You are going to be a leader in modeling God's love.

To be different, we must choose to practice God's different kind of love!

BE A I CORINTHIANS 13 LOVING LEADER!

Summary

- Biblical love comes from God alone.

- Biblical love is a command, not an option.

- Biblical love is sacrificial not self-focused.

- Biblical love is practical (I Corinthians 13):

  - Love suffers long.
  - Love is kind.
  - Love envies not.
  - Love vaunts not itself; is not puffed up.
  - Love does not behave itself unseemly.
  - Love seeks not her own.
  - Love is not easily provoked.
  - Love thinks no evil.
  - Love rejoices not in iniquity.
  - Love rejoices in truth.
  - Love bears all things.
  - Love believes all things.
  - Love hopes all things.

For Consideration and Action

- Look at the characteristics of genuine Christian love from I Corinthians 13. Do you demonstrate this type of leadership?

  - The patient, non-defensive leader—"suffereth long"
  - Looking-to-be-useful-in-someone's-life leader—"is kind"
  - The non-jealous leader—"envieth not"
  - The small, unapplauded leader—"vaunteth not itself; is not puffed up"
  - The courteous, non-offensive leader—"doth not behave itself unseemly"

- The unselfish, giving leader—"seeketh not her own"
- The non-explosive leader—"is not easily provoked"
- The forgiving leader—"thinketh no evil"
- The pure leader—"rejoiceth not in iniquity, but rejoiceth in the truth"
- The covering leader—"beareth all things"
- The believes-the-best-about-others leader—"believeth all things"
- The never-give-up leader—"hopeth all things"
- The never-quit-leader—"endureth all things"

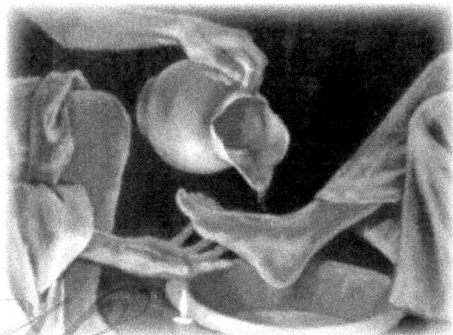

How can I be a different kind of leader?

Chapter 8

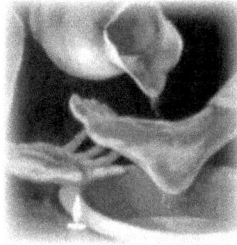

DIFFERENT CHOICES

by Ken Collier

T he eight-year-old boy and his six-year-old brother were having a few choice words in the den. Apparently, one had left the favorite chair unattended, presumably to return in a few moments. However, his brother spotted the empty chair and laid claim to it. Dad heard the opening shots being fired and ventured onto the carpeted battlefield to mediate. This happened in my home, but I am sure that, with a few minor adjustments to the script, this scene has been played out in other homes as well.

Some years before this event, I had coined a little expression based on a diagram I had studied at a counseling conference. It was a simple concept, and my hope was that my children would use it to make choices that would please the Lord. The rhyme went this way:

> *Just two choices on the shelf,*
> *Pleasing God or pleasing self.*

When I, as the referee, had quieted the "mob," both boys had a pretty good idea what was coming: "Boys, Dad is going to ask you both the question. Were you pleasing God by what you were saying to your brother just now, or were you pleasing yourself?" The question itself is almost always convicting. They were wrong, and they knew it. They admitted that there was nothing loving towards God or each other in the scene that had just happened. In order to please God, both boys had to admit their selfishness both to God and to each other. Each had to ask forgiveness of God and of his brother for his own actions and words. In addition, each had to ask forgiveness from God for the selfish heart's desire that wanted to have its own way more than it desired to love God and others. All of this happened on the prompting of a single reminder that with every choice we are going to be pleasing someone, either God or self. After all was handled, one boy went one way, the other went the other way—and the three-year-old got the chair!

Actually, cases involving our choices to please God or self are never closed for any of us, are they? A leader who wants to be different on purpose must be a leader in making choices that are different from those around him. How many choices do you make in an average day? That is a preposterous question with no definitive answer. Who knows? Could we safely say hundreds, perhaps thousands? Life is made up of choices and our choices, singly or linked together, will actually change the direction of our lives.

When one makes a choice, he is "selecting something with a goal in mind." When I choose to get up on time or, perhaps, to hit the snooze button, I am making a selection with a goal in mind. One goal might be to grab 15 more minutes of sleep. The opposing goal could be to get up promptly so I will have enough time for my personal time with the Lord. One choice favors me. The other choice favors my God. Many times it is just that simple, but simplicity does not imply that the choice is easy. *(There are) just two choices on the shelf, pleasing God or pleasing self.*

Since it is true that every choice shows preference for something or someone, it would make good sense that a godly leader is a person who makes godly choices and uses his influence to teach others to do the same. Here are a few things for the godly leader, one who wants to be different on purpose, to consider:

I Must Make Personal Choices That Please God

We must challenge our own everyday choices. There is no way we can assume that, being left to ourselves, we will generally choose to please God! The Scripture warns us of our tendency to go our own way instead of God's way. As godly leaders, we must continually recognize the crossroads represented by our many daily decisions, and we must consciously choose to please God by obeying the commands and principles of Scripture. "Kicking it into neutral" is not the way to make choices that please the Lord.

> *He that trusteth in his own heart is a fool, but whoso walketh wisely, he shall be delivered.* Proverbs 28:26

> *For all seek their own, not the things which are Jesus Christ's.* (Philippians 2:21)

> *There is a way which seemeth right unto a man, but the end thereof are the ways of death.* (Proverbs 14:12; 16:25)

> *Every way of a man is right in his own eyes: but the Lord pondereth the hearts.* (Proverbs 21:2)

It would do each one of us a great deal of good to stop and consider the choices we are making each day. Our choices must square with Scripture. We must "think Bible." We may be surprised to discover that we have stopped challenging decisions about which we were once careful. We may begin to think that our choices please God simply because we have endeavored to walk with the Lord for many years. We could begin to think that our choices must naturally please Him. A good leader challenges even the seemingly small choices in his life to see if they truly please God. He asks, "Am I pleasing God by saying this or doing this? Or am I pleasing myself?" There **are** just two choices!

I remember being impacted as a teenager by the book *In His Steps* by Charles Sheldon. I realize that the now-familiar WWJD ("What would Jesus do?") question comes from this old book; however, it is still a timely question. Not only is it the essential direction in biblical decision making, but it also provides a serious caution. The issue is "What would Jesus *do*"; it is not what we *feel* that Jesus would approve. Allowing feelings to dominate would mean that anybody's interpretation of what Jesus would do is as good as anyone else's. However, Christ the Living Word has revealed in His written Word how we are to make choices that follow His will for us. We are not left to our subjective feelings: God has given us clear, objective commands and principles.

I Must Challenge the Wrong Choices of Others

It may sound bold, but we cannot stay neutral when friends and associates around us are making choices that are not in keeping with the principles of Scripture. Godly leaders are different in that they are called upon to challenge the choices of others. Consider the following verses:

> *They that forsake the law praise the wicked: but such as keep the law contend with them.* (Proverbs 28:4)

> *Brethren, if a man be overtaken in a fault, ye which are spiritual, restore such an one in the spirit of meekness; considering thyself, lest thou also be tempted.* (Galatians 6:1)

He that saith unto the wicked, Thou art righteous; him shall the people curse, nations shall abhor him: But to them that rebuke him shall be delight, and a good blessing shall come upon them. (Proverbs 24:24-25)

He that rebuketh a man afterwards shall find more favor than he that flattereth with the tongue. (Proverbs 28:23).

The godly leader challenges the wrong choices of others.

I Must Instruct Young-but-Growing Christians In Right Choices

Right choices are not learned by giving children independence at the earliest age possible. Right choices are learned as young Christians watch older Christians handle choices and challenges in a godly manner. As we go about our routine tasks, we should make it a practice to have with us young people, young church members, and young associates in our ministries. Our goal is to challenge them to think through choices that they will be required to make one day. People are out there who are willing to learn. We need to find them and train them! Coaches spend much time recreating a game-like atmosphere in order to teach players how to respond in actual games. The godly servant-leader is always eager to teach as he goes about his daily routines. This was the manner of our Lord with His own disciples, and it was the method of the Apostle Paul with many individuals in the early Church; therefore, it is an outstanding method that we should be practicing today. Do we take advantage of the opportunities to train and influence the young, growing Christians around us?

That ye may approve things that are excellent; that ye may be sincere and without offence till the day of Christ. (Philippians 1:10)

And the things that thou hast heard of me among many witnesses, the same commit thou to faithful men, who shall be able to teach others also. (II Timothy 2:2)

In summary, godly leaders make God-pleasing choices and encourage others to do likewise. Do not just fly through the intersection of choices. Take time to "think Bible" so that you will be able to give the pattern to those who follow you. Thomas J. "Stonewall" Jackson, a strong Christian, did this. His wife records these comments of his:

I have so fixed the habit in my own mind that I never raise a glass of water to my lips without lifting my heart to God in thanks and prayer for the water of life. Then, when we take our meals, there is the grace. Whenever I drop a letter in the post office, I send a petition along with it for God's blessing upon its mission and the person to whom it is sent. When I break the seal of a letter just received, I stop to ask God to prepare me for its contents, and make it a messenger of good. When I go to my classroom at the Virginia Military Institute and await the arrangement of the cadets in their places, that is my time to intercede with God for them. And in every act of the day I have made the practice habitual.

Just two choices on the shelf, Pleasing God or pleasing self.
HONOR GOD WITH YOUR CHOICE!

Summary

- Just two choices on the shelf: pleasing God or pleasing self.

- We must make personal choices that please God. (Think Bible—Proverbs 28:26; Proverbs 14:12; Proverbs 21:2)

- We must challenge the wrong choices of others. (We cannot stay neutral—Galatians 6:1; Proverbs 28:4; Proverbs 28:23)

- We must instruct the young and the growing Christian. (Philippians 1:10; II Timothy 2:2)

For Consideration and Action

- Consider the statement, "Life is made up of choices and any number of choices singly or linked together could literally change the direction of my life." Are you able to illustrate the truth of this in your own life?

- Today challenge yourself to slow down when you come to choices and challenge them to make sure they please God by matching with Scripture. Do this for one third of a day and see if choices may be modified.

- Are you actively involved in teaching younger Christians to make decisions in a way that pleases God? Name two people with whom you are consistently close enough that they notice the pattern by which you make decisions. Discuss this pattern with them.

- Is there an individual involved in self-pleasing decision patterns whom you should challenge to please God?

Chapter 9

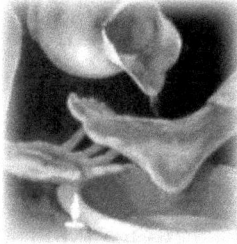

DIFFERENT ATTITUDES AND ACTIONS

by Matt Williams

I n order to become a different kind of leader, we must have different attitudes and actions in our lives. What is the key to open the door of change? Let's look at several verses dealing with change, considering what they have in common:

> *Whosoever believeth that Jesus is the Christ is born of God. And everyone that loveth Him that begat loveth Him also that is begotten of Him. By this we know that we love the children of God when we love God and keep His commandments. For this is the love of God that we keep His commandments, and His commandments are not grievous.* (I John 5:1-3)

> *If you love me, keep My commandments.* (John 14:15)
> *Ye are My friends if you do whatsoever I command you.* (John 15:14)

These are just a few verses that show us the key to the victorious Christian life—*change by obedience, that is, giving our wills back to God.* As stated in an earlier chapter, Romans 12:1-2 says, "I beseech you therefore brethren by the mercies of God that ye present your bodies a living sacrifice, holy, acceptable unto God, which is your reasonable service. And be not conformed to this world, but be transformed by the renewing of your mind that you may prove what is that good and acceptable and perfect will of God." God wants us to give Him our bodies, minds, and wills.

God's Word Is Our Final Authority

If we are created to glorify God, we must use God's Word as our authority in making decisions in life. We live in the days of talk shows on radio and TV, and everyone seems to have an opinion about everything. But, for the Christian, God's Word is our final authority. Our actions and attitudes must line up with His standard.

Actions Based on Past Experience Are Not Wise

A few years ago I was approached after a Sunday morning service by a lady who was visiting our church. She asked if I would come to a local public school where she taught and be a guest speaker in her class. It had been a few years since I had been in a public school, and this sounded like a great opportunity. I told her I would be happy to come. She let me know that the topic was divorce and remarriage. "That will be fine," I replied, "but I will use the Bible as my text." She said she understood and believed we would have a good discussion. I went to her school and did have a good class. Here is what happened. She opened up the topic, and hands began to go up. Students were eager to share their experiences with divorce and remarriage, telling what had happened in their own families or in other families. They also shared their opinions about divorce and remarriage. Their statements began with words such as, "Well, I think...." As the class continued, I had the opportunity to share what God's Word said concerning the subject. It was a special time as this group of public school teenagers focused on God's standards regarding marriage.

We all have opinions, experiences, and ideas, but for the Christian, God's Word must be our *final authority*. It is our standard, sent from God. If we make decisions based only on our experiences and opinions, we are no different from the lost world around us.

What are the effects of our choices? Consider II Peter 1:4 on the effect of one specific category of God's Word, the promises of Scripture: "Whereby are given unto us exceeding great and precious promises. That by these ye might be partakers of the divine nature, having escaped the corruption that is in the world through lust." These promises bring us into the best that God has to offer and provide a safeguard against destruction.

Actions Based on Natural Reasoning Are Not Wise

Abraham, in the book of Genesis, learned some great—and terrible—lessons in this area. He was a man of God, but in Genesis 13 he made a decision based on his logical reasoning. There was a famine in the land, and he left God's will to go to Egypt. His decision, based on his natural opinion, led to spiritual harm for Abraham himself and for others. There was another situation in Genesis 16 where he received wrong counsel and made a decision to have a child by Hagar, the handmaid. This again was a decision based on human reasoning and not on God's plan. God wanted to supernaturally provide a son for Abraham.

God's Word is our final authority in whatever we do with our lives.

I beseech you therefore, brethren, by the mercies of God, that ye present your bodies a living sacrifice, holy, acceptable unto God, which is your reasonable service. And be not conformed to this world: but be ye transformed by the renewing of your mind, that ye may prove what is that good, and acceptable, and perfect, will of God. (Romans 12:1, 2)

Trust in the Lord with all thine heart; and lean not unto thine own understanding. In all thy ways acknowledge him, and he shall direct thy paths. (Proverbs 3:5-6)

II Peter 2:19-21 evaluates the condition of the Christian who has escaped the pollutions of the world but becomes entangled in them again: *"It would have been better to have never known the way of righteousness."*

Actions Based on Watching Others Are Not Wise

We are to compare ourselves, not to others, but to God's Word. II Corinthians 10:12 declares, *"For we dare not make ourselves of the number, or compare ourselves with some that commend themselves: but they measuring themselves by themselves, and comparing themselves among themselves, are not wise."* One of the blessings of Christian fellowship is to have the encouragement and testimonies of others around us. But we cannot base decisions just on what others do or tell us to do. We must use the Word of God as the primary standard for our actions.

God's Love Is Our Standard

In John 15:12 God says, "…love one another, as I have loved you." There are five characteristics of Jesus' friendship demonstrated to us in chapter 15 verses 13-16.[3]

1. The extent of His friendship is sacrificial love (v. 13). A man may have no greater love than to die for his friend, but the Son of God died for his enemies to make them His friend. Am I demonstrating this kind of friendship, even to those who are not friendly toward me?

---

[3] From *Quality Friendship: The Risks and Rewards,* by Gary Inrig, Moody Press, 1999.

2. The effect of His friendship is change (v. 14). Friendship is not conditional, but it is transforming. What observable effect is my friendship having on my friends?

3. The expression of His friendship is intimacy (v. 15). Have I verbally expressed *to* my friend my love and appreciation *for* my friend.

4. The initiative of His friendship is His love (v. 16). Am I an initiator of love, or am I waiting for others to reach out to me?

5. The goal of His friendship is fruitfulness (v. 16). We are to go and bear much fruit. How am I helping my friend to realize his potential in every area of his life?

A New Freedom

As we discuss actions and attitudes, the word *freedom* often comes up. Some Christians say that we have the freedom to do whatever we want to do. As I see Scripture, the freedom is not to do whatever *we want* to do, but we have a new freedom to do what *God wants* us to do. This freedom is not *license*. It is *liberty* in a sense parallel to the expression, "freedom of motion" that might describe one whose physical abilities are restored after being damaged by disease or injury. Before I put my faith and trust in Jesus Christ at the age of twenty-four, I did not have that freedom. In fact, one of the things that used to frustrate me was that the older I got, the harder I seemed to try, and yet my actions and attitudes were getting worse. I could compare myself to others on a secular college campus and say that I was better than most people. I got up and went to church every Sunday; very few did that. I kept myself pure, true. Yet in many other areas I found that I was not doing as well as I used to do. In Christ I have a new freedom because I am not in the bondage of sin. We have a brand new freedom to do what God wants us to do.

Making Choices by the Commands of Scripture

Let's take a look at this freedom. There is much to say in Scripture about our actions and attitudes. According to I John 5, if we love God we will keep His commandments.

Some years ago I taught Bible in our Christian school. I really enjoyed the class. One of the things that I used to do every year was to come to class one day and say there were certain issues that some people say are wrong for Christians to do and others say are okay. I would ask them to list some of those issues. It was interesting because, for about seven or eight years in a row I did the same thing, and the students came up with the same topics each year. Then I would divide up the class into small groups and say, "Let's see what Scripture says about these particular issues." When they searched, it was amazing to see how much these students could find in God's Word about these questionable areas. God's Word does have much to say specifically about the actions and attitudes in our lives.

I often draw a circle on a board to explain biblical freedom. Inside the circle I write that word, *freedom*. At the top of the circle I write the word, *commands*. At the bottom of that circle I write the word, *principles*.

Commands

Principles

The Christian has freedom in Christ. This freedom is the ability to do what is right. Before becoming a Christian I did not have this freedom: I was in the bondage of sin. I was frustrated because, even though I was trying harder to be a "good person," I was falling backwards, bound by sin. Through the power of God, Christians have the freedom to do what is right according to the commands and principles of Scripture.

Besides the commands of Scripture, there are many principles given to us. Let's take a look at these principles.

Making Right Choices by Principle

The Bible has many clear, situation-specific commands, such as "Thou shalt not bear false witness," or "Honor the Lord with the firstfruits of all thine increase." In addition to the commands of Scripture, the specific *do*'s and *don't*'s, are the principles of Scripture, which tell us how to approach many situations. The following are a few very helpful principles.

Whatever I do should be a help to my life

I Corinthians 6:12 states that "all things are lawful unto me, but all things are not expedient." I Corinthians 10:23 repeats that idea, ending with the statement that "all things edify not." Something might be lawful but not helpful. Golf, for instance, is certainly "lawful," but pouring one's life into developing a golf swing—getting things out of balance—can be a waste of life.

Whatever I do should not get me in its power

The second part of I Corinthians 6:12 says that "...all things are lawful for me, but I will not be brought under the power of any." Will this action become controlling in my life? Sports, reading, physical fitness, dieting, computers—there is no end of things which are harmless or even good for us, as long as they are kept in balance. We must beware, though, that these things do not begin to bring us under their power. Is there any "good" thing in your life that often pushes other good and necessary things out?

These first two principles relate to my responsibility to my own life. The next principle relates to my responsibility to other Christians.

Whatever I do should not cause others to stumble

I Corinthians 8:9-13 provides an example of this principle. The problem was whether Christians could buy certain meat offered in the marketplace. It was probably good and inexpensive, but it had been sacrificed to idols in the heathen temple. Paul acknowledged that an idol is "nothing," and could not affect the meat. He also acknowledged that, for some who had just been saved out of a heathen background, the association of that meat with temple worship could draw them back into other elements of that lifestyle. See how Paul balances Christian liberty with Christian love: *"But take heed lest by any means this liberty of yours become a stumblingblock to them that are weak. For if any man see thee which hast knowledge sit at meat in the idol's temple, shall not the conscience of him which is weak be emboldened to eat those things which are offered to idols; And through thy knowledge shall the weak brother perish, for whom Christ died? But when ye sin so against the brethren, and wound their weak conscience, ye sin against Christ. Wherefore, if meat make my brother to offend, I will eat no flesh while the world standeth, lest I make my brother to offend."* Our action may not be sinful in itself, but it may influence someone else, who believes that it is sinful to violate his conscience.

The last principle relates to my relationship to God Himself.

Whatever I do should bring glory to God

I Corinthians 10:31 states, *"Whether therefore ye eat, or drink, or whatsoever ye do, do all to the glory of God."* This is the ultimate consideration. Is the glory of God my primary motivation, and is it the actual effect of my choices and of my influence upon others?

Therefore, I have responsibilities to myself, to other Christians, and to non-Christians.

Guidelines for Manner of Life

As these five principles indicate, no Christian lives just for himself. All the more, the Christian leader must consider how his actions affect others. Romans 14 is the great passage on the "Law of Doubtful Things." Again, the specific problem was whether or not the Christian could eat meat that had been sacrificed to idols. Although the problem is ancient, the principles of this passage have been a real help to me in trying to decide what is right for me to do today. Let's look at six principles given here.

1. If we do something that other Christians don't, we are not to belittle them: "Let not him that eateth depise him that eateth not." (v. 3a)

2. If others do things that we don't, we are not to judge them, or to treat them as bad people: "…and let not him which eateth not judge him that eateth." (v. 3b)

3. I am to be fully persuaded that what I do is right for me to do: "Let every man be fully persuaded in his own mind." (v. 5)

4. What you do will affect others: "For none of us liveth to himself, and no man dieth to himself…. It is good neither to eat flesh, nor to drink wine, nor any thing whereby thy brother stumbleth, or is offended, or is made weak." (vv. 7 and 21)

5. You must give an account to God of your own actions, not the actions of others: "So then every one of us shall give account of himself to God." (v. 12)

6. We must do things to build up others " Let us therefore follow after the things which make for peace, and things wherewith one may edify another." (v. 19)

Let's look at an application of these principles. Let's say that you decide not to have a television in your home because of the many bad programs. However, someone else in your church decides to have a television, but keeps close control over what is watched. Romans 14 is telling you to be fully persuaded about what is right for yourself to do. If you do certain things and believe, according to Scripture, that you have the freedom to do them, and others choose not to, you are not to belittle or despise them. If others do things that you don't, such as having a television, you are not to judge them. Let's say there is a third person that chooses to have a television and has no standards whatsoever as to what the family watches. Does that person have that freedom? According to Romans 14 he does not. These principles can be a help to us in making our own decisions without looking down on or gossiping about others. When I found this passage years ago it was a great help to me in choosing my actions and in seeing the freedoms that we have in Christ.

Remember, this freedom is the ability to do what God wants us to do, not the license to do whatever we choose.

Biblical decision making
Enables one to make a difference for good:
DECIDE TO MAKE A DIFFERENCE!

Summary
- Actions must be based on God's Word as our final authority.

- Actions based on past experiences are not wise.

- Actions based on our own reasoning are not wise. (Proverbs 3:5-6)

- Actions based on watching what others do are not wise.

- God's love must be our standard in making choices.

  ○ Make choices by the commands of Scripture.
  ○ Make choices based on the principles of Scripture.

For Consideration and Action
- Do you use God's Word as your authority in the choices that you make concerning your actions? Mediate on the principles from I Corinthians 6, 8, and 10 concerning making right decisions by principle.

- Do you find that you often base your actions on experiences that you've had or on your own reasoning or opinions? Think of an example of a choice that you made in the past. Analyze how much the decision process was based on Bible principles.

- Do you battle making choices based primarily on what others do or on what others think that you should do? Look over the four principles on making right decisions by principle. Can these be a help in making decisions now concerning an action or a choice that you must make?

- Consider the guidelines for manner of living. Do we find ourselves belittling others or judging others? Mediate on the principles from Romans 14 regarding how we should regard those who differ from our standards.

Chapter 10

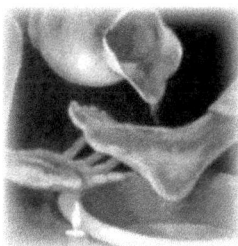

A DIFFERENT WAY OF HANDLING PROBLEMS

by Matt Williams

Proverbs 16:20 says, "He that handleth a matter wisely shall find good: and whoso trusteth in the Lord, happy is he." Often, these "matters" are those opportunities in disguise: problems. This Scripture gives us a good perspective on handling problems the biblical way. A problem well handled can be a blessing because it opens the opportunity to trust God for His way of solving it, rather than leaning on our own understanding. This trust, in turn, puts us in the place of God's blessing. The following ten principles can be a major help in our lives in dealing with problems that come our way.

Principle #1—*Show that you love God by doing what He says*

By this we know that we love the children of God, when we love God, and keep his commandments. For this is the love of God, that we

keep his commandments: and his commandments are not grievous.
(I John 5:2-3)

The principle is to show that you love God by doing what He says. It is one thing for us to come to church on Sunday morning, maybe even to come to Sunday school or a Bible study. We can learn, we can grow, and we can say that we really want to love the Lord; but we *show* that we love Him by obeying Him. When a problem arises, am I proving that I love God by how I handle it?

As a young Christian I faced a decision concerning music. I was getting involved in church and working with young people when God began to speak to me about the music that I was listening to. I was reading in I Samuel 16:23, which said that when David played his harp for Saul, two things took place. 1) his spirit was refreshed, and 2) he recovered and was made well. I had to ask myself whether those things took place when I listened to my music. The answer was no. My spirit wasn't being refreshed and I wasn't recovering spiritually because of the music that I was listening to. I had a choice to make. Was I going to obey God or do what I wanted to do? This principle is a very important one for victory in the Christian life. Galatians 1:10 says, "For do I now persuade men or God?" Many times we are making decisions because we are more interested in pleasing ourselves or other people than we are in pleasing and obeying God.

Principle #2—*Just say no*

My son, if sinners entice thee, consent thou not. (Proverbs 1:10)

The principle is a simple one—just say no. Now, we've all heard of slogans and programs encouraging people to "just say no" to drugs, but this principle goes further. It is telling us that, if others try to get us to do wrong, we are to be more concerned about pleasing God than we are about pleasing them. We are to say no. In fact, Proverbs 1:10-14 provides advanced warning on the "three tactics of enticement."

1. The tactic of involvement—we want to be included.
2. The tactic of inducement—we are being persuaded by elements that seem very attractive and exciting.
3. The tactic of entanglement—we become active participants.

Steer clear! God gives the warning signs, and He expects us to act:

Cease, my son, to hear the instruction that causeth to err from the words of knowledge. (Proverbs 19:27)

I will set no wicked thing before mine eyes. (Psalm 101:3)

Years ago when I was the administrator of our school, there were three young men going home after a basketball game one Friday night. The idea came up to "farm Dave's yard." Dave was a student in our school; they were all in the senior class. *Farming,* to some people in the country is to take a plow and get ready to plant a field. To us city slickers, however, it means to drive through someone's yard and leave an impression on the lawn. The three seniors thought it would be a great joke for Dave to walk out the next morning and notice that someone had farmed his yard. I would have to say they weren't the three most intelligent seniors that we've ever had at our school. But they were good guys from good Christian homes. On this occasion they were not using great reasoning. You see, first of all, it had been raining, and the ground was very soft. They should have been considering the consequences—but they weren't. And, sure enough, they got stuck in Dave's front yard: the wheels sank into the soft ground. The second consideration that they did not make was that Dave's front yard had an underground sprinkler system. In their efforts to get out, they caused several hundred dollars worth of damage to the system.

On Monday I had to deal with the young men. Normally I would ask questions like "What did you do? What should you have done? What will you do next time?" Those are good questions to ask, but for some reason I deviated from the normal approach. The first student came in. He had no idea what I knew about the Friday night escapade. I asked him what he did on Friday night. He was apparently trying to guess, "Does he know or does he not know?" He was thinking through all the possibilities. It finally came out that he had farmed Dave's yard. Then I asked that question that I normally don't ask. "Why did you do it?" Here was his reply: "I don't know. I didn't really want to do it, but the other guys acted like they wanted to do it, so I went along with it." I told him what he needed to do now: they needed to apologize to Dave's family and pay for the sprinkling system.

I called for the second individual. Same questioning. It finally came out—he had farmed Dave's yard. Again I asked the question, "Why did you do it?" Interestingly enough it was the same reply. "I don't know. I didn't really want to do it, but the other guys acted like they wanted to do it, so I did it." Again, I went through what needed to be done.

Then the third young man came in. He would have to be the culprit—the one who had initiated the action. First of all, he was driving; and, secondly, he came up with the idea of farming in the first place. I asked the same questions. "What did you do Friday night?" It finally came out—he had farmed Dave's yard. And again I asked, "Why did you do it?" Interestingly enough, he had the same reply. "I don't know. I didn't really want to do it, but the other guys acted like they wanted to." In fact, he said, "It was my idea, but, as soon as it came out of my mouth, I knew it was a bad idea. But, they seemed so excited!"

Here were three guys from three good Christian homes. If just one of those three had said no, I am convinced that it would have saved much difficulty. The principle is just to say no when we are confronted with a situation that is against God's Word or the authorities in our lives. By saying no to wrong choices and to people who are promoting them, we are saying that we are more interested in pleasing God than in pleasing ourselves or other people.

Principle #3—*Watch out for red flags*

A prudent man foreseeth the evil, and hideth himself; but the simple pass on, and are punished. (Proverbs 27:12)

What is the *simple fool*, in the sense used in the book of Proverbs? It is someone who acts now and thinks later. The principle is to watch out for signs of spiritual danger. But the simple just do not see them. We have all seen these simple fools—so caught up in self and in attracting attention that not much thought goes into actions. This reminds me of a college experience. I had only been there for a few weeks when I began to think what a wonderful place it was. The college campus had two gyms, all kinds of activities, a student union, and a snack shop to go and drink Dr. Pepper's; it was great! The only problem was that I had to attend class. I began to daydream about what it would be like to go to college and not have to go to class. In fact, I had a schedule all figured out. In my daydream I was the only one that didn't have to go to class. Everyone else did. I would get up early in the morning. Other students would be getting up early to go to class, and I would go eat breakfast with them. After breakfast I would hang around the dorm. I would go to the Student Union by mid-morning and drink Dr. Peppers with some of my friends. Come back for lunch. Have a little nap after lunch. Go in and shoot hoops for a while in the afternoon. Come back to the dorm and have dinner. Go out on a date. Watch TV, and then go to bed. I thought, "Wow, what a great place! If I went to college and didn't have to go to class it would be wonderful!"

I spent four years at that secular university. In my senior year I began to hear a rumor. There was a new rule that had just been made: seniors were not going to have to take final exams. That meant I would have one week while everyone else was taking final exams, and I would not have to go to class, but I would be on campus. This was my dream come true! I was so excited! And just as in my daydream, I began to carry out the proposed schedule in that final week. I got up early, ate breakfast, and saw the others who were taking finals off to class. On and on the schedule went. But, you know, I'd really have to say that after about a day and a half of my schedule, it wasn't as exciting as I thought it would be. In fact, by the afternoon of the second day I became a little bored. Things got so bad that by Tuesday evening there was a group of six seniors who were playing *Clue* down in the lounge of our dorm. Now, there is nothing wrong with *Clue*; it is a wonderful game, but here I was on this campus with all these wonderful things to do, and I was playing *Clue* in the lounge with a group of other bored seniors. Just about that time a so-called friend of mine came in and said, "Hey, Matt, come with me."

I said, "Where are you going?"

"It's going to be great!" he said. "We are going to paint the dean of men's name on the street."

The dean of men was an odd person. I had never really talked to him, but every once in a while he would come around and check up on what was going on. I could just envision him seeing his name painted on the street downtown in this university town. But the more that I thought, the more questions came to mind. In fact, I had this picture, this impression on my mind of a lady in a sweatshirt with the letters "M—O—M" on the shirt.

It was my mom! I knew that if I painted the dean of men's name on the street and word ever got to her, I would be grounded for half of my life. I wasn't a Christian yet, but still there was something in me that said Mom would kill me if she found out. So, I stayed back, and my so-called friend went on. He came back in about 45 minutes. He had been caught by the dean of men while painting the dean's name on the street! He ended up getting expelled from school. He had attended four years, had passed every class, and all he had left was graduation practice. Yet he did not graduate because of this foolish action—and I came very close to going with him. There are Christians that act before they think and violate this principle all the time. The key is to watch out when our conscience is raising red—or even yellow—flags. Before you act, think through the possible consequences.

Principle #4—*Let God cover sin*

He that covereth his sins shall not prosper: but whoso confesseth and forsaketh them shall have mercy. (Proverbs 28:13)

The principle is that we should not hide our sins, but we should let God cover sin in His way. One Bible term for forgiveness translates literally as "to cover." It carries the picture of the blood of Christ covering our sins. When we do wrong, our tendency is to lie, or at least to avoid the truth, to cover up for the wrong. Then we lie to cover up for the lie, and on and on it goes. God tells us that, if we cover our sins, we will not prosper, but if we confess and forsake them, He will give us mercy. This is a very important principle.

Years ago when I was teaching in our school a young man came into my office and said, "Pastor Williams, I have something to share with you. Yesterday we had a Bible test, and I cheated on it. I just couldn't sleep last night. I felt so bad about it. I know I deserve an F. It was wrong of me, and I just had to tell you about it." At this point I wanted to have mercy on that student. I said, "You really do deserve an F. That was wrong of you, and not only was it a sin against God, but it was also a sin against the class because of others that studied diligently for the test. I tell you what I'm going to do. Tomorrow, if you will come in early, I will give you a test. Not the same test. That wouldn't be fair, but I will give you a brand new test. Whatever you make on that test will be your grade. Is that fair enough?"

Boy, had I gained a friend! He thought he was going to receive a failing grade for the first test, and now he had a second chance. He was very thankful. As far as I know, he never cheated again. I just wanted to give some mercy.

Now, if I want to do that, how much more does God want to show mercy? I am not saying it's always going to work out just that way, but God says that He will give mercy. That's even more important than the mercy we can give. This is a very important principle—*Let God cover the sin.*

Principle #5—*Keep a clear conscience*

And herein do I exercise myself to have always a conscience void of offense toward God and toward men. (Acts 24:16)

The principle is that, when we do wrong, we should immediately seek to make things right with God and, if it applies, with the people offended. Now what does that mean to have a clear, or clean, conscience? It means you are able to look anybody in the eye and say that there is no problem which you have not tried to make right between you and that person. God says we are to have a conscience void, or empty, of offense not only toward Himself, but also toward other people. He also says in Matthew 5:23-24, "If thou bring thy gift to the altar and there rememberest that thy brother hath ought against thee; Leave thy gift before the altar, and go thy way; first be reconciled to thy brother, and then come and offer thy gift."

Principle #6—*You can't stay neutral*

They that forsake the law praise the wicked, but such as keep the law contend with them. (Proverbs 28:4)

Our responsibility to edify one another as believers has two aspects. We often hear about our responsibility to encourage one another; we do not mind that. But there is a second side. It's one we don't like to hear much about. When a brother is in sin, we have a responsibility to help him to see his problem. The principle is this: if you fail to stand up for what is right, you are failing God and man. It doesn't mean that we have a license to go and confront everybody on every little thing that goes on, but I think that we realize when something is serious enough that we need to confront a brother or sister. It is easy to say that confrontation is the pastor's job, and, yes, pastors do get involved in that. However, God wants every believer to be involved in this ministry, as well.

You can't stay neutral. You are either for something or you're against something. There is really no neutral ground. Often the Christian community is good at praising and encouraging and building up one another, and that is good. But there are times that we have to go and confront someone in love because of something that is taking place. It is not an easy thing to do, but it's a biblical thing to do. Matthew 18 tells the procedure of confrontation, and Galatians 6 focuses on the kind of spirit that we must have for any such confrontation. It is very, *very* important that we have both the right attitude and the right actions. Without these we will not be the biblical leaders God wants us to be.

Principle #7—*Silence can mean approval*

He that justifieth the wicked and he that condemneth the just, even they both are an abomination to the Lord. (Proverbs 17:15)

Some people say that bad is good, and some say that good is bad, and God hates both of these perversions. This switching of labels is not done only by the radically wicked of society; it is more common than you might think, and it often occurs in our Christian circles. If someone is doing wrong, he naturally wants to defend his actions. Or, someone does right, and somebody else—even a family member or fellow church member—criticizes him or her for it, perhaps because the critic feels uncomfortable with the contrast between the right choice and his or her own position. God says that if we say that bad is good or that good is bad, both of those things are an abomination. Can we remain silent and allow that which God hates to go on? The principle is that failure to challenge a wrong action can mean approval or can be misinterpreted as approval, having the same bad effect. There really is no neutral ground. If we remain silent, we are more interested in the approval of the wrongdoers than in the approval of God.

A couple of years ago a young lady told me about what took place when she went to a Christian college. She had two roommates; one was a junior, and one was a sophomore. She was the freshman. After being in the room for a few days, she noticed that some of the conversation was not very Christ honoring. But who was she, the lowly freshman, to say something about the language. She just put up with it. After a couple of weeks, while getting ready for bed one evening, she thought of this principle—silence can mean approval. She got out of bed and looked up Proverbs 17:15. She realized what she had been doing was an abomination to the Lord and she determined that she was going to seek to help the situation. The next day she came back to her room, and there were her two roommates. She shared with them how God had convicted her about the language in the room and that she wanted to apologize for her part. I thought this was a good way for her to approach it. Even though she could honestly say that she did not partake in the communication, in their eyes, by being silent, she was just as guilty as they were. They probably could not remember who said what at which time. After that it got very quiet in her room, and the roommates didn't say anything for the rest of the evening. She thought they were mad at her. The next day after class she came back into the room, and one of the girls was there. As soon as she entered the room, the girl ran up and gave her a hug and said, "Thank you for what you shared last night. I have been feeling bad about our conversation as well, but I didn't have the courage to say anything about it." She told me that the language in the room was much better for the rest of the semester. Here was a freshman that had made a difference for her two roommates—one a junior and one a sophomore—by applying this principle. God's Word really does work.

Principle #8—*Give your friends a choice*

A friend loveth at all times, and a brother is born for adversity. (Proverbs 17:17)

Open rebuke is better than secret love. Faithful are the wounds of a friend; but the kisses of an enemy are deceitful. (Proverbs 27:5-6)

By standing for right we are giving others an opportunity to choose right. This is the principle of giving others not only encouragement to do right, but also a positive alternative. This is the other very positive side of that difficult task of confronting sin.

A few years ago we were having a Student Leadership Conference in Kansas City. A school administrator called me with a problem. He wanted students to come to the conference, but he could get only two students to come, one girl and one boy, and he did not have a sponsor to send with them. I said that I would love to have them come and that we would put them in with another group so that they would be able to participate in the group activities.

I saw them throughout the week. They were rather quiet, but they seemed like nice kids. Nothing about them attracted any particular attention. Yet, later on, I heard a story from their school administrator about what had taken place in that young man's heart.

As usual, I shared the principles that you can't stay neutral, that silence can mean approval, and that you should give your friends a choice. All the while, God was really challenging this young man to make a difference back at his school. There was a situation about which I, as the speaker, could not have known. He was on the school basketball team. In the locker room rock music was being played on someone's boom box before and after practice. The conversation was gutter language. He didn't like it, but he had remained silent. He did not think he could really do anything about it so he had decided to remain neutral. God challenged him at the Leadership Conference that he should go home and really seek to make a difference on that basketball team.

He accepted that as an assignment from the Lord. He arrived home on a Thursday evening, and the next day he went to basketball practice just like every other night. When he got there, he found the same music and the same gutter language going on. He got up on the bench in the locker room and said, "Guys, can I have your attention?" Somebody turned off the boom box. He said, "Guys, the Lord has just really convicted me about some of the things that are taking place here with the music and language."

One of the other players said, "Oh, just sit down and shut up! Who do you think you are? You just went off to this conference and you think you're so spiritual." Then a few other guys began to chime in. He got down off the bench and went to practice.

After practice he went into the locker room, got changed, went into the coach's office, and said, "Coach, I want you to know that I appreciate you and appreciate being on the team, but I'm not going to be on the team anymore. Just want you to know that there are some things going on, and I don't believe I can honor the Lord and be a part of the team."

That was the end of practice on Friday night. Monday night he did not go to practice. The administrator said that by Tuesday night, the entire team came over to that young man's house begging him to come back on the team. They promised him that if he came back on the team that there would be no more bad music, no more gutter language, and that they would really seek to do right. As I listened on the phone I was thinking, "Wow, that guy must have been some kind of basketball player. The team must have expected to lose the rest of the games for the season." Then the administrator said this courageous young man was only a sophomore and hardly ever played. He sat on the bench most of the time.

And then it clicked. This was the impact of a young man who gave his friends a choice. It was the impact of a young man who said, "I'm not going to be silent about wrongdoing anymore." Initially, yes, some stood against him, but through Monday night and Tuesday conviction was setting in. The administrator told me that for the rest of the season things went great, and the team really sought to honor the Lord. One sophomore high school student changed the course of that entire team for that season just by giving his friends a choice.

We have no idea when we stand for right, or when our children stand for right, how much impact it has by giving others a choice to stand for right as well. To me, one of the blessings of being in a good Bible-believing church, and, for students, being involved in a good Christian school, is the fact that there is a positive peer pressure. Not everyone does right all the time, but there is leadership that is going a biblical direction. There are others that want to do right, and they just need someone to encourage them. As they stand for right, others will go along with those who believe God enough to exercise biblical leadership.

Principle #9—*Discipline is good, not bad*

Smite a scorner and the simple will beware. Reprove one that hath understanding and he will understand knowledge. (Proverbs 19:25)

When the scorner is punished the simple is made wise and when the wise is instructed he receiveth knowledge. (Proverbs 21:11)

The principle is that God intends to help and heal through discipline. As hard as discipline is, both in the giving and in the receiving, we must remember that God has designed it for good. Discipline is not fun as a parent. It is harder still in the school situation. Church discipline is so hard that many churches outright ignore God's command, and they lose the blessing of God on their work. Still, we have to realize that God has allowed that discipline, and that it is good. First of all, it is good for that person. Secondly, it's good for others. It's good for others because that is when the simple will beware. The simple will see what happens to a wrongdoer and think, "I'd better think before I act." It helps them to make wise decisions and not get involved in some things that are taking place.

Principle #10—*Two or three can help*

Two are better than one because they have a good reward for their labor. For if they fall, the one will lift up his fellow, but woe to him that is alone when he falleth for he hath not another to help him up. (Ecclesiastes 4:9-12)

To me, one of the great things about being involved in a church is that we can be a part of helping others. Someone comes in and he needs a friend. This person may be a new Christian needing a friend to help him to stand, and we can be that friend or we can get him with someone else that can be his friend. What a blessing that is! This is the principle of fellowship. The principle that two or three can help.

When I was a young Christian, at first I didn't know if there were any other Christians at work. It did not take me long to find out. All I had to do was pray before I ate, and others approached me and let me know that they were Christians also. Interestingly enough, one of the men was someone that, before then, I did not think I liked very much. He was not offensive; he was just a little different. However, when I got to know him, I really began to like him. He and another employee were having Bible study once a week before work, and they invited me to join them. They were a great help and a great encouragement to me.

Two or three helped me, even in the work situation. In addition, I had the church that I was getting to be involved in. As we look at this principle, first of all we must realize that God does not intend for us to be Lone Rangers; He wants us to be encouraged by others. Secondly, though, we must realize our calling to be a help to other people. Who needs a friend? Maybe there's a new Christian at work. Maybe there's someone that you can just reach out to in Jesus' name, Yes, it takes time, it takes care, but what a blessing it is to both give and receive encouragement in the Lord.

In life we will have problems, but each problem is a chance for God to show the wisdom of His Word and the superiority of the Christian life. These ten principles, just ideas pulled straight from the Bible, provide proven ways to see the blessing of God in the problems of life.

Problems are inevitable. How we handle problems
REFLECTS OUR COMMITMENT TO GOD.

The case studies in Appendix 1 provide lifelike situations in which these ten principles for dealing with problems should be applied. Individual consideration or group discussion of how to handle these situations is valuable preparation for meeting the real problems you will face.

Summary

- Ten principles for handling situations wisely (Proverbs 16:20):

  - ° Show you love God by doing what He says. (I John 5:23)

  - ° Just say no! (Proverbs 1:10)

  - ° Watch out for red flags. (Proverbs 27:12)

  - ° Let God cover sin. (Proverbs 28:13)

  - ° Keep a clear conscience. (Acts 24:16)

  - ° You can't stay neutral. (Proverbs 28:4)

  - ° Silence can mean approval. (Proverbs 17:15)

  - ° Give your friends a choice. (Proverbs 17:17)

  - ° Discipline is good, not bad. (Proverbs 19:25)

  - ° Two or three can help. (Ecclesiastes 4:9-12)

For Consideration and Action

- What two or three principles given in this chapter are the greatest struggles for you in your decision making?

  - ° Memorize and mediate on the verses that go with those principles.

- Is there a situation that you are currently facing in which one of these principles can help in your choice?

- Is there someone you know that one of these principles can help in his or her decision making? Are you willing to share it with that person?

- Is there someone that needs to be confronted concerning a situation, but you've stayed away from handling it? Are you willing to be a biblical leader by seeking to help?

Chapter 11

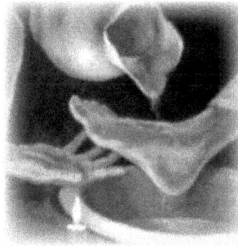

A DIFFERENT HOME

by Ken Collier

T he teams I choose to cheer for tend to be notoriously slow starters. They begin the game almost lethargically and generally get in a hole that is too deep to climb out of. Another thing I have noticed about my teams is that they tend to lose often. I wonder if we have hit upon a correlation? Undoubtedly, we have. Slow starters make it rough on themselves. I will continue to be loyal to my teams, but it would be easier on the stomach and the win / loss record if they started out well.

Godly leadership begins in the home. In this arena of life, above all others, the godly leader must start off well. The home of the servant leader should be victoriously different from the average home. The home is the beginning point for the good things that happen in all the other arenas of life. It is a grievous thing to talk to the children or the spouse of one who is heavily involved in ministry and hear the sad words, "I know what people think he's like at church, but he's a totally different person at home." That is the wrong kind of difference for sure.

Personal Integrity

Abraham, Moses, Joseph, Daniel, Boaz and David were men of integrity. Similarly, Sarah, Ruth, Deborah, Abigail and Mary were women of integrity. Studying through each of these lives, one cannot avoid being affected by the fact that each of these people exhibited the same basic character and love for God in every situation with which they were faced. Yes, we see notable lapses in Abraham, David, and others. These lapses warn us along the way, but, after all was done, we see lives of integrity. I heard an excellent definition of integrity that states, "Integrity exists when one part of your life faces another part of your life, and they both say the same thing." The penultimate Faithful Witness, God the Father, made a startling statement about Job. Job 2:3 says, *And the LORD said unto Satan, Hast thou considered my servant Job, that there is none like him in the earth, a perfect and an upright man, one that feareth God, and escheweth evil? And still he holdeth fast his integrity, although thou movedst me against him, to destroy him without cause.* Although they were imperfect humans, this is the type of character that made these men useful to God in their lifetimes.

The ultimate Man of integrity is our Savior, Jesus Christ. Never do we see Him contradicting His own character. We have the privilege of following His life closely in Scripture and we are amazed at His righteous consistency. This is what we should aim for as servant leaders. Even when the Jewish leaders paid witnesses to testify that Jesus had spoken falsely, the false witnesses could not agree. The "prince of this world cometh and hath nothing in me," said Christ. That 12-year-old boy that honored His earthly parents at the feast was the same young man who honored His Heavenly Father by going to a cruel cross. *Jesus Christ, the same yesterday, and to day, and for ever* (Hebrews 13:8). That is integrity.

Ultimately, He is our model. He was the same servant wherever He went. When one part of our life looks at another part of our life, do they both say the same thing? Can it be said of us that we are the same patient people at work as we are at ball games? Are we the same gentle people at home as we are at church? Are we the same ones in our standards with friends at work as we are with friends at church? Are we the same kind of people behind the wheel of the car as we seem to be when visiting an ailing person at the hospital? Does our family say we manifest the same gentleness and patience at home with them as we do with our friends or the church leadership? A person who has lost integrity at home, work, or church cannot function as a true leader after the image of Christ, our model of integrity. What area of your life needs to be brought into conformity with the spirit of Christ, the Man of integrity? Since the home of the servant leader must be different, perhaps it would be good to review a few of the areas that make the home of God's servant leader different.

A Different Home Means Having a Different Goal

The home of the servant leader has in it the goal of pleasing God by becoming like Christ. The home is unified because each family member, as he comes of age, understands that the one household goal that a Christian can never lay aside is that of pleasing God by becoming like Christ. *For whom he did foreknow, he also did predestinate to be conformed to the image of his Son* (Romans 8:29). In my opinion, the most powerful and practical explanation of the process of change is the book *Changed Into His Image* by Jim Berg. It is a "must read and re-read" for the family! It is never too late to establish that the home is the place where each family member wants to please God. Each family member wants to be like Christ. Many of the questions children ask and the applications adults can give in the growing up years center around this goal of the home.

Amos 3:3 asks, *Can two walk together, except they be agreed?* It is critical that the goal of the home be in alignment with God's goal for each of His children. Confusion will surely result if a family member chooses popularity or money over God's established goal of pleasing Him by becoming like Christ. Joshua made a bold statement,... *but as for me and my house, we will serve the Lord* (Joshua 24:15d). That statement was not made on the spur of the moment. There was, no doubt, reinforcement, long discussions, application, and even discipline behind Joshua's statement. Establishing the goal is a beginning for any family that is different on purpose.

A Different Home Means Each One Doing His Job

Am I talking about house jobs like doing the dishes, washing the clothes and feeding the pet? No. I mean each one must delight in submitting himself to the responsibility God has given him in the home. That means submission to God's authority and submission to any authority God sets up in the home. Who delights in submitting to authority? For one, Jesus Christ delighted in it. Even His earnest prayer in the garden brings us to this conclusion. Matthew 26:39 says, *And he went a little further, and fell on his face, and prayed, saying, O my Father, if it be possible, let this cup pass from me: nevertheless not as I will, but as thou wilt.* Obedience and submission to His Father's plan were characteristic of the life of Christ, and it is destined to be characteristic of ours also. In John 8:29 Christ states, *And he that sent me is with me: the Father hath not left me alone; for I do always those things that please him.* Briefly stated, here is the "delightful" job description for each member on the household in the home that desires to be different.

Each one submits to each other

Ephesians 5:21 says, *Submitting yourselves one to another in the fear of God.* Each family member should be in the frame of mind to "yield right of way" to any other family member at any time. This is capturing the spirit of Christ presented in Philippians 2:3: *Let nothing be done through strife or vainglory; but in lowliness of mind let each esteem other better than themselves.* Each family member believes that the needs of every other family member are more important than his own. Is this the normal way of a family? No. It is the goal of a family of servants who desire to be different as Christ was different. He considered the needs of others to be more important than His own needs.

Wife submits to her own husband

Ephesians 5:22-24 gives the wife the "job" of submitting to her husband, just as she would to the Lord. Actually, that is her way of submitting to God. She is showing her love for her God by submitting to one who, oftentimes, is not worthy of this. However, she is sacrificing for her God in her submission. Later, in verse 33 of the same chapter, she is told to reverence him. That sounds difficult! That sounds different! And, truly, it is. That is why it is necessary to have the grace of God that is behind the command. The wife must "do her job" with delight for she does it "as unto the Lord." She will lead and impact her family and others by her submission to her own husband.

Husband loves his wife

In Ephesians 5:25-30, the husband is instructed to love his wife as he does his own body. He is to lead her in such a way that, when she stands before the Lord at His appearing, she will not be ashamed. This is quite beyond the man's ability to do, but that is the job of every husband and father who would desire to be different as God counts difference. This can only be approached by a man who is indwelled by the Holy Spirit and is walking in Him.

Children obey and honor parents

In Ephesians 6:1-3, we find the very familiar job of the children. Each must obey and honor his parents "in the Lord," that is, as he would obey and honor the Lord. This is a big job, but no one can do it for the child. It is his way of demonstrating his love for, and his trust in, his God. He needs God to be able to do this. Even so, young people can lead and impact others by their example of honoring parents.

Parents bring up their children

In Ephesians 6:4, the parents are to *provoke not [their] children to wrath*, but are commanded to *bring them up in the nurture and admonition of the Lord.* Easy task? No way! It is a big job, but they must do it. They cannot do it alone. They need God. Parents who bring up children in God's order are fit to be followed in other relationships. They are leaders who make a difference.

It seems simplistic to say, "Just do what the Bible says," but ultimately, this is what must happen in the home of the one who would be different on purpose. Because we delight to submit to the authority of God, we willingly submit to His plan for the home. Coaches and employers, whether Christian or not, say simply, "Just do your job!" That's it. That is what must be done in the home. Delighting in authority is right to do!

A Different Home Means a Home Full of Servants!

Servant leadership is the topic of this book. The best practice for any servant is the home. It means that dad is always ministering by doing the "next thing that benefits his wife, teaching her more of the grace of God" (Mark 10:43). It means that a brother is serving his sister and doing the "next thing that will make her successful in God's eyes" (Mark 10:44). It means a home that has the atmosphere of serving, ministering, and giving as Jesus Christ did in His home in Nazareth

(Mark 10:45). A home can be dramatically different if each family member adheres to Philippians 2:3-4: *Let nothing be done through strife or vainglory; but in lowliness of mind let each esteem other better than themselves. Look not every man on his own things, but every man also on the things of others.*

Having the heart of a servant is an attitude of life. The sweetness of the Spirit of Christ the Servant lives where servants dwell. In the home that has chosen to be a fellowship of servants, one would think up an act of kindness for his family members and be disappointed to find out it had already been done for him! Our homes may never reach that ideal, but they can be growing in that direction by God's grace. Even a child can serve. Being a servant is the privilege of practicing the "mind of Christ" (Philippians 2:5-8). That is a different way to live. That is leading by being Christ's follower.

A Different Home Means a Home Filled with Godly Love

A different kind of love makes its presence known in the home where servant leaders live. A loving home means there is a willingness to sacrifice for the benefit of another. Godly love is supernatural, so it requires the grace of God to function. This kind of love is a command of God; therefore, it is activated by our obedience. How does godly love look in the home? It looks practical and kind.

Biblical love is a gift every day,
But you express it in practical ways.

Here are some possibilities for the home that is different because love abounds:

1. Husband gets up early and adjusts the temperature to a comfortable level for the family.

2. Son gets up without having to be reminded and comes to breakfast early.

3. Wife prepares an occasional special breakfast.

4. Daughter asks if she can iron someone else's clothes while she is touching up her own.

5. Dad comes home from work and helps the kids do their review work for the test.

6. Son thanks mom for the meal and volunteers to do the dishes.

7. Daughter volunteers to get a "little one" ready for bed.

8. Husband calls wife from work for no obvious reason… just because!

9. Mom anticipates the upcoming school project, buying the materials and having them on hand.

10. Husband asks the question about how the day went before the wife has a chance to ask the question.

11. Brother and sister each play the other sibling's favorite game.

12. Daughter is kind to mom's friends on the phone and takes accurate phone messages.

13. Dad initiates a family round-table discussion when the same problem resurfaces over and over.

14. Each family member leaves small notes of encouragement for the others or spends time picking out funny cards.

15. Husband goes shopping with wife. (This is extravagant love!)

16. Father and son are careful with manners at the table, not having to be reminded.

17. Son mows the lawn or washes the car without being asked.

18. Husband turns down the volume on the TV or radio news and lays aside the paper in order to hear his wife's or his child's question or comment.

19. Son or daughter volunteers to baby sit so that mom and dad can date one another.

20. Husband repairs something in the house that aggravates his wife.

21. Dad has devotions with the family.

22. Daughter asks mom if there is something special she can pray about.

23. Dad takes son or daughter on a date or an out-of-town ministry trip.

24. Mom chauffeurs the children with a rejoicing spirit.

25. Each takes the smallest, worst, and dirtiest for himself.

If things are as they should be, the man will be the pacesetter for love in the home. The home will be different because godly love is not natural, but supernatural in its results. It is pleasant to follow a leader who comes from a home wherein everyone is doing his or her job as a husband, a father, a wife, a mother, a brother, a sister, or a child. This is the kind of home where joy, laughter, and enjoyment of each other makes family members eager to be together anywhere, anytime.

A supernatural difference produces supernatural joy:
REJOICE IN THE TASK GOD GIVES YOU!

Let's get practical. Appendix 2 provides four lists of simple, everyday ways to be a servant in the home. These are suggestions of ways that the husband can serve his wife, that the wife can serve her husband, that parents can serve their children, and that children can serve their parents.

Summary
- Integrity of life is the condition in which "one part of your life faces another part of your life, and they both say the same thing."

- The home of a godly leader is different in its character, marked by the following:
  - Each family member's goal is to become more like Christ through obedience to God's Word.
  - Each family member faithfully does his God-ordained "job."
  - Each family member strives to serve the other family members.
  - Each family member's actions are regulated by Biblical love.

- Biblical love is a gift every day, but you express it in practical ways.

For Consideration and Action
- Would your family say that you have a life of integrity? Do they see you as being the same person at home, at church, and at work or school?

- Ask each family member what he believes is the goal of your family.

- Ask each family member what he believes is his God-given "job" in the family and what that means to him each day.

- List three things you could do for each family member that would express sacrificial, godly love during busy times of life.

Chapter 12

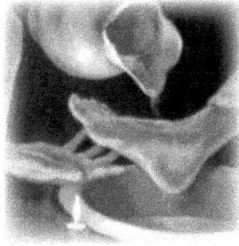

DIFFERENT RELATIONSHIPS

by Matt Williams

S cripture gives us not only commands and principles to live by, but also illustrations of people who were obedient and disobedient to those commands and principles. We can learn from their lives. One such individual was Matthew. He was not just unpopular: he was despised. He worked for the Roman government even though he was Jewish, and, even worse, he worked as a tax collector. He made his income by cheating and overcharging. It was a good job financially, but socially it was the worst of trades. He was the person that no one else liked. One day while Matthew was working at his collection station, Jesus came to him and said, *"Follow me"* (Matthew 9:9). Scripture says that he immediately rose and followed the Savior. From that moment on, he was a transformed person. In the past, however, he had offended and used many people. So, one by one, he had to make restitution for all the wrong he had done.

Through Matthew's life we can discover some tremendous principles for establishing right relationships and restoring ones that have been broken. We do not live our lives in a vacuum. We must have relationships with others. Romans 14:7 says, *For none of us liveth to himself, and no man dieth to himself.*

Every day we are called upon to relate to people: our families, our friends, our teachers, our co-workers. This is where our Christianity really shows—in the way that we relate to others. If it doesn't work there, something is wrong. Let's take a look at what God says about these different relationships.

Relationships with Family

Our families have a tremendous influence on us. In fact, the way that you feel about your family and the way you act toward them shape a great deal of your personality. It carries over and determines how well you relate to others. It also has a great deal to do with your future, including your success in marriage. Unresolved conflicts with parents have a strange way of turning into conflicts with spouses and children. You cannot compartmentalize your life. Relationships in one area affect every other area sooner or later. You cannot isolate your family life from your social life or neatly divide your spiritual life from your school or work life. They are all interrelated and draw upon each other in both strengths and weaknesses.

That is why God is interested in relationships. It all begins with the family. He set up relationships there in the beginning. He is deeply interested in how we carry them out. The Bible not only gives us God's ideal for the family, it also shows how each member of the family should function.

It all begins with the instruction to children in Ephesians 6:1-3: *Children obey your parents in the Lord: for this is right. Honor thy father and mother; which is the first commandment with promise; That it may be well with thee, and thou mayest live long on the earth.* Colossians 3:20 adds another element: *Children, obey your parents in all things: for this is well pleasing unto the Lord.* The little phrase "in the Lord" is very important. Some would have you believe that you have to obey your parents only if they are Christians, but that would contradict the original and broader statement in the Ten Commandments. Others say it means that obedience is required only in spiritual matters, or only if the parents are right. Neither of these is what God had in mind, because Colossians says, "in all things." We are to obey our parents because they are representatives of the Lord Jesus Christ. *A mature attitude can only be developed by learning how to properly respond to authority* (Ephesians 6:1-2). In fact, Romans 13:1-7 tells us that one who resists authority resists God and receives condemnation.

What about parents? Ephesians 6:4 tells us that parents are to nurture, not to provoke, children. It is a huge responsibility to be involved in the process of nurturing our families.

Perhaps nurturing can best be explained by an illustration. Imagine a huge piece of marble a sculptor has chosen to make into a beautiful statue. At first the stone is rough, uneven, and not very pretty to look at, but the sculptor does not dwell on that. He sees in that piece of marble what it is going to become. So, he picks out his tools and begins to work, hammering, chiseling, and polishing until the rock has been shaped and finished into a beautiful statue.

All of us are like that piece of marble. We are not completely smooth or finished. There are rough edges and some dull spots, but we have the possibility of being formed into a beautiful likeness—the likeness of Jesus Christ. And, like the marble, there must be some work done on each of us. So God, the greatest of all artists, raises His tools and begins to chip away the rough, hard edges, and to sand and polish the dull edges. He is making you like His Son. And what are the tools that He uses? Two of the chief tools in the life of a child are a father and mother. Other tools are teachers, pastors, bosses, and others in authority over us.

God warns us over and over in Proverbs that only misery and failure can follow one who despises or rejects, cares little for, or counts as nothing, his parents and their instruction (Proverbs 15:20, 23:22, and 30:17). That is God's plan for the home. Christ is over all; and the father and mother lovingly shape the children into the image of Christ for their good.

Relationships to Authorities Outside the Home

God gives a plan for adults as well as for children.

1. Surrender your rights—Colossians 3:22. *Obey in all things your masters....* I believe there are two fitting words under this vital principle, *honor* and *loyalty*. Honor is the attitude of seeking to make those over us successful. Loyalty is speaking up for someone or something. It is unswerving allegiance. That should be our attitude toward authorities in our life.

2. Serve with sincerity—Colossians 3:22. *In singleness of heart....* The two words to consider here are *cooperation*, doing all that we can to be a help to others around us, and *support*, seeking to help others and to allow the Master to be successful in the lives of those around us.

3. Serve wholeheartedly—Colossians 3:23. *And whatsoever ye do, do it heartily, as to the Lord.* Two key words here are *impartiality* and *love*. Impartiality is serving all, not just some that I like, around me. Love is giving of myself to meet the needs of another and expecting nothing in return (I Corinthians 13:4-8).

Five Guiding Principles

Scripture presents five vital principles about our relationship to authority.

1. It is ordained of God—Romans 13:1-2

2. All are under authority—Hebrews 13:7

3. Be a servant to those over you—Ephesians 6:5-8

4. Be especially thankful for Christian authority—I Timothy 6:1-2

5. Each must give an account for his actions and attitudes—Hebrews 13:17

In conclusion, I must remember to honor the position of those over me, even if at times I disagree with the personality.

One last word for children: independence is not demanded, but earned. If you want more adult privileges, you must show more adult behavior.

Relationships with Peers

We have considered principles concerning our relationships with our families and with the authorities over us. God also gives us the great responsibility to be an encouragement to other Christians around us.

Our friends are probably the most important group of people in our lives, outside of our families. Whether adult, teen, or child, we spend a great deal of time with friends. This can be at church, school, work, or even at home, but, wherever it is, we spend a great deal of time with friends. Let's take a look at the levels of friendships and the responsibilities that come with each level.

Who our friends are should not be determined by our choosing. Our friends should be those who will accept us and our commitment to the Lord. *"Blessed are ye, when men shall hate you, and when they shall separate you from their company, and shall reproach you, and cast out your name as evil, for the Son of man's sake"* (Luke 6:22). If we stand for the Lord's principles, we will not have to leave wrong friends: they will leave us.

Levels of Friendship

Level 1: Acquaintances—Based on General Associations

The first level of friendship is our acquaintances. We normally do not think of these as friends, but they are; and we have a responsibility to them. These are the people we see occasionally, and with whom we have conversations on very general topics. We talk mostly about public information: the weather, work or school, sports, and what is happening in our community. We all have acquaintances. Our responsibility is to show Christian love.

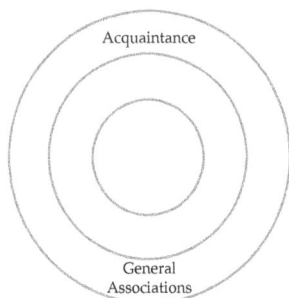

Our Responsibility to Acquaintances: To Show Christian Love.
(Galatians 6:10; Proverbs 18:24) There are many ways to show Christian love.

- We are to be friendly, cheerful, and have a countenance that shows the joy of the Lord. Smile!
- Meet new people. Show an interest in them and their lives.
- View each person you meet as someone that God has sent your way.

Galatians 6:10 says to do good unto all men, especially unto those who are of the household of faith. Our acquaintances should know us as "good doers." On this level, first impressions are important. That friendly, cheerful smile can be a real avenue of ministry. By our very countenance we can attract people or scare them away. When you are around people, look for new faces, people you do not already know. We often get absorbed in our cliques without realizing it. At church, we shouldn't always be with the same people and ignore those that we do not know. We are cheating them and ourselves out of some possible new and genuine friendships. When you do meet a new person, make a special effort to remember his name and to greet him when you see him again. Be a good listener. This is why it is so helpful to have already thought out questions and concentrate on the answers given to you. One of the most sincere compliments that you can give a person is your undivided attention.

Level 2: Casual Friendships—Based on Common Interests

The second level of friendship is casual friendships. These are people with whom we have a common interest. We may live in the same neighborhood; we may go to the same church or school; or we may work in the same place. With these people we have a little more freedom. We talk about opinions, ideas, and possibly even some goals in life. Because we have spent more time with these people we can talk more about spiritual things.

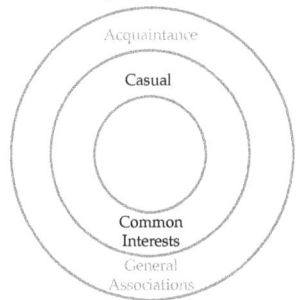

Our Responsibility to Casual Friends: To Develop Christian Love

Our responsibility here is to develop Christian love. Hebrews 10: 24 says that we are to *provoke [one another] unto love and to good works.* We should initiate opportunities and give the other person the chance to respond. When we have spent time with a person sharing activities and common interests, we have earned the privilege of sharing more with him: personal qualities, characteristics, interests, opinions, and goals. Here are some keys to ministering at this level:

- Be an honest, sincere friend. Don't use people for your gain.
- Through conversation, find out the other person's goals in life.
- Discern whether you should spend more time with him and become closer in friendship.

If he should share a problem with you, it is important that you reflect interest and genuine concern. Now is the time to simply share how you found the answer to your problems in Jesus Christ. Be honest about yourself and, with discretion, share some of your faults and problems if it seems appropriate. No one will be shocked to discover that you are not perfect, and in many instances, your honesty about yourself opens more doors of opportunity.

I Samuel 23:17 says that Jonathan *went to David...and strengthened his hand in God.* David was at a very discouraging time in his life. His friend recognized this and took the initiative of being a friend—a true biblical friend—by strengthening him spiritually.

Level 3: Close Friendships—Based on Common Goals

People often think that Christians must have only Christians as their friends. In a sense this is true, but as we have already seen, acquaintances and casual friends can either be Christian or non-Christian. It is an opportunity to show Christian love and to draw people, whether saved or not, closer to the Lord. The third level of friendship is close friendship. In this friendship your life goals must be the same. It is based on a harmony of spirit. Therefore, it is vital that close friends are going the same direction.

A result of this common direction is brotherly love. John 13:34-35 states, *A new commandment I give you that you love one another. By this shall all men know that ye are my disciples if you have love one toward another.* One of the greatest attractions of Christianity is genuine Christian love.

Our Responsibility to Close Friends: To Strengthen Christian Love

Proverbs 27:17 also states that *Iron sharpeneth iron; so a man sharpeneth the countenance of his friend.* In close friendships we must strengthen Christian love. The relationship begins with discovering a person's goal in life to know if we can become close friends. As the friendship deepens, we help our friend reach those goals. Along the way, it is vital to encourage, uplift, and pray for that friend.

Proverbs 13:20 says, *He that walketh with wise men shall be wise, but a companion of fools shall be destroyed.* Close friendships are vital in helping us to become what God would have us to be.

Once you have learned that a person knows Christ as his Savior and wants to live for Him, you can discover and discuss specific goals, his ministry, and God's plan for his future. You can assume a personal responsibility to do everything that you can to help him reach those goals. If you know your friend is interested in music, you can keep him alert to opportunities to use his talent and improve it. Train yourself to think of "projects" you can design to help him reach his goal. Be alert to Scriptures that would encourage or guide him and share them with him. So often we have close friendships with other Christians and yet are not having true fellowship in helping one another meet God's purpose.

There are many things that we can do to help encourage and strengthen others. Perhaps the best way to begin is to look at our own lives and start working on projects that will help us move closer to Christ. We can share with our close friends what God is doing in our lives and what we are learning from His Word. This can be tremendous fellowship.

On this level we even have the freedom to correct one another in love. You have discerned his strengths and faults, and he has discerned yours. Now you can search the Scriptures and help each other grow in areas where growth is needed.

As the close friendship grows, specific responsibilities grow with it.

- You are committed to faithfulness to each other, safeguarding each other's reputation.

- You are always available to each other for help, comfort, and rejoicing.

- You have a mutual freedom to correct one another in love.

In conclusion, as we consider Christian friends, there are five areas of responsibility that we should consider:

1. Be a giving friend (Galatians 6:10; Philippians 2:4).

2. Be a building friend (Hebrews 10:20; 4:25; Psalm 34:3; Ephesians 4: 29; Proverbs 27:17).

3. Be a peace-making friend (Matthew 5:9; Psalm 133:1).

4. Be a loyal friend (John 15:25; John 13:34-35).

5. Be a restoring friend (Galatians 6:1-2; Proverbs 27: 6).

Principles for Dealing with Christians in Sin

Unfortunately, we need to consider relationships with those who claim to be Christians, and yet are not following God's Word.

Christians are to avoid unnecessary relationships with professing Christian's of evil character (I Corinthians 5:11). They are not to keep company with them because evil companionships corrupt good morals and character (I Corinthians 15:33). *He that walketh with wise men shall be wise, but a companion of fools shall be destroyed.* (Proverbs 13:20).

Christians are to avoid close relationships with those whose minds are on earthly things (Matthew 6:19-34). This sometimes can be a difficult situation. You must really have your eyes on Christ and be willing to suffer some misunderstanding and even rejection from those who do not understand your goals and purpose in life. There are three commitments you need to make in these all-important relationships.

First, purpose that those who reject Christ must reject you. This does not mean that you go out of your way to see that they reject you; they must be rejecting you for the Christ they see in you. The Scriptures warn us to keep company only with those who approach God in sincerity. This term, *to keep company,* refers to spending optional friendship time, fellowshipping, or hanging out with someone. It does not refer to the necessary and non-optional relations of work, school, and so on. If an acquaintance shows no interest in the things of the Lord or pretends an interest just to keep your friendship, you would be better off not spending significant amounts of time with that person. Other people may keep away from you because they see you spending so much time with people who have negative values and goals. This is especially important in dating relationships. You may not want to break off a relationship with someone not interested in spiritual things, but you have no idea the number of others that are looking at your relationship with that individual and are not coming to you for friendship because of it. God does not want you to ignore acquaintances and unsaved friends, but the warning still stands. The different types of friendship carry different responsibilities, and it is dangerous to confuse them. Most of your time should be spent with those who approach God in sincerity.

God knows the powerful influence of one's peer group. He knows the intense pressure on a teen who wants to be liked like everyone else—to be accepted and admired. We must be very careful that our peer group influences us to the good, wholesome, and pure things in life, and not to the fleshly side of our own natures. Proverbs 28:7 states, *Whoso keepeth the law is a wise son, but he that is a companion of riotous men shameth his father.* Proverbs 3:19 warns of people *whose end is destruction, whose God is their belly and whose glory is their shame, who mind earthly things.* The prime object in life for these people is, essentially, thrills, laughs, and popularity—things that yield only selfish gratification. They find humor in shameful things. These are the people who tell smutty jokes or who laugh at them, who make fun of spiritual matters, and who find pleasure and satisfaction in the impure. "Their glory is in their shame." They are not living for the future—only today. The fact that tomorrow brings the consequences of their actions means nothing to them. They operate only on an earthly, temporal value system—they "mind earthly things." There is no room for the spiritual, eternal values in their life. They are all caught up in the now, the flesh, and the "I." These are the kind of people you are turn from. These are the fools, the riotous men that Proverbs warns about. Ask God to help you to become sensitive to the character qualities of people so that you might be aware of wrong friends and not become entangled with them. This must be the first commitment that you make in the area of friendship. Those that reject Christ cannot be your close friends.

Second, purpose ahead of time to verbally identify with Christ if you are asked to violate a Bible conviction, and think through how to do this in such a manner as to glorify God and to help even the one you must oppose. Some people have no problem with the *purposing* or the *verbally indentifying* part of this, but they have about as much grace as the proverbial bull in the china shop about the *manner* in which they do it. And the sad thing is that they are doing more to turn others away from Christ than to draw them to Him by their method. Let us say that a teenager is offered a cigarette by one his acquaintances. On the part of the one offering the cigarette, it was probably a friendly gesture. To draw back in horror and gasp, "Oh no! I wouldn't touch one of those nasty things! I am a Christian!" would be wrong. A better answer is "No thanks, as a Christian I don't believe that I can honor the Lord and smoke." Can you sense the difference? The personal offense is gone. You still verbally identified with Christ, you have still made him aware of the difference between the two of you, but you have made the grounds or basis of that difference less offensive. It is simply that you have made a decision that he has not, whether the decision be deliberate on his part or not. But whatever his response is, you must refuse to get angry or to let any ounce of spiritual pride rise to your face or voice. In all things communicate a genuine interest and acceptance of the person.

Third, purpose to let God choose your friends on the basis of their needs and their openness to your help. If you have been working with someone who shows no willingness to accept the Gospel, but still wants to be your friend, be very careful not to ignore him completely. Just don't allow the friendship to move into the level of "close friendship." This is where being involved at church can really come in handy. Do not give up any church activities to spend time with him; instead, invite him to come with you. Let him know what God is doing in your life. Your commitment to the Lord and His work will either communicate the importance of having Christ in one's life or it will convince him that he does not want to be around you. The convicting work of the Holy Spirit can spark his interest and draw him back far better than your own efforts. And remember; never stop talking to God about this person and his needs. Pray for him and let him know that you pray for him.

Relationships with the Lost World

The Christian's Purpose for Dealing with the Lost

There is an overriding principle in John 17 relating to our relationships to non-Christians, the principle of mission. We, as believers, are sent to the world (John 17:18-19). This is our purpose. We must continually remind ourselves that our goal, our purpose in life, is that we are sent to the world. Two key statements are made in this passage. 1) In verse 17 Christ says, *Sanctify them through Thy truth: thy Word is truth.* We are to allow God to sanctify us so that those who hear might be sanctified by the Truth. 2) Then, in verse 21, He states the goal: *They all may be one; as Thou Father art in Me, and I in Thee, that they also may be one in us: that the world may believe that Thou has sent Me.* One of the greatest results of the unity of the believers is its powerful testimony for winning the lost to Christ. We are to be one in Christ so that the world might see and believe. People are watching us whether we realize it or not.

The Christian's Principles for Dealing with the Lost

Two overriding principles need to be considered as we talk about our relationship to the world.

First, Christians are to avoid close relationships with non-Christians (II Corinthians 6:14-16). We discussed this earlier. We can have acquaintances and casual friends; we are to be with them; but we cannot become close friends with those who have different objectives and goals in life.

Second, Christians are not to avoid necessary relationships with non-Christians (I Corinthians 5:9-10). We are around them, and God has spoken clearly on His goal for our associations. Our mission is to be His agents of reconciliation. Too often we get so caught up in our own Christian lives, our families, our church, and all of our activities that we forget that there are hurting people around us. Don't avoid the necessary relationships. Let's pray daily as we go into the world that we might be the salt and light that God has called us to be. I Peter 3:15 tells us to sanctify the Lord God in our hearts and always to be ready to give an answer to anyone that would ask a reason for the hope that is within us. Our daily prayer as we go into the world, rubbing shoulders with the world, should be that we might impact the world.

Every relationship has its God-given responsibilities:
REMEMBER WHY YOU ARE HERE!

Summary

- Your attitude can only be developed by learning how to properly respond to authority. (Ephesians 6:1-2; Romans 13:1-7)

- Who your friends are should not be determined by your choosing. Your friends should be determined on the basis of who will accept you, your life, and your commitment to the Lord. (Luke 6:22)

- There are levels of friendships and responsibilities with each level.

  - Your responsibility to acquaintances is to show Christian love. (Galatians 6:10)

  - Your responsibility to casual friends is to develop Christian love. (Hebrews 10:24)

  - Your responsibility to close friends is to strengthen Christian love. (Proverbs 27:17)

- The Christian has a relationship to Christians who are not living for the Lord.

  - Christians are to avoid unnecessary relationships with professing Christians of evil character. (I Corinthians 5:11)

  - Christians are to avoid close relationships with those whose minds are on earthly things. (Matthew 6:19-34)

- The Christian and his relationship to the lost

  - Christians are to avoid close relationships with non-Christians. (II Corinthians 6:14-16)

  - Christians are not to avoid necessary relationships with non-Christians. (I Corinthians 5:9-10)

For Consideration and Action

- How do you respond to the authorities in your life?

- Who are your acquaintances? Do you show Christian love to them? How do you show it? Are you seeking to build that friendship on a higher level, if possible?

- Who are your casual friends? Are you seeking to develop Christian love by being an honest, sincere friend? What could you do to improve the relationship?

- Are you faithful to your task of spiritually strengthening close friends?

- Do you have any close friends that are not Christians? What should you do if this is the case?

- Look over the principles for the Christian in his relationship to other Christians. Are you avoiding unnecessary relationships with professing Christians of evil character?

- Are there some Christians with whom you should avoid closer relationships because their minds are on earthly things?

- Are you too close to some non-Christians as evaluated by time spent with them and by their negative influence on you?

- What can you do to be a help to them without hurting your own testimony and your walk with the Lord?

Conclusion

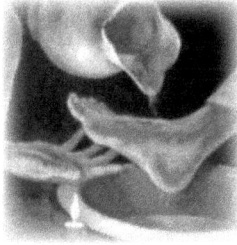

ATTRACTED TO JESUS CHRIST

by Matt Williams

I grew up as a Roman Catholic in a religious home. Where we lived in the St. Louis, Missouri, area, everyone seemed to be Roman Catholic. We really did not know much about Protestants. I think there was one on our block, but all I knew about how Protestants were different from Catholics was the fact that they went to church longer than we did. I would go to church with my mom for the six o'clock mass—that is 6:00 *in the morning*—and be home about 7:00. I could go back to bed, have a little nap, get up, eat breakfast, go outside and play for a while, come back in, eat lunch and go out again, and they *still* weren't home from Sunday school and church. What in the world were they doing?

I will never forget a discovery I made when I was a junior in college. One night, as I was on a date in a downtown area, we walked past a storefront church, and the church was having an evening service. I had never heard of an evening service. I thought, "What are they doing in there? Are they left over from the morning, or what is this?" It was totally foreign to me.

But I made another, more important, discovery in that junior year when I met a certain young lady. We were serving on a committee together, planning activities, and I saw a difference in her life. I thought I had everything that you were supposed to have in organized religion. But she had something different, something that I did not have. I asked many questions, and it took me a little while to understand. Many times I would ask her why she did certain things or why she did not do certain things that other people were doing at this secular college. Each time she came back with a Bible answer, and that really impressed me. She would ask me why I did certain things. Usually I had to answer, "I don't know. I never really thought about it." I saw that I had no basis for my decisions.

On spring break when I went home, I dug out all my religion books, trying to figure out why I was doing certain things that I was doing. Because of the influence of one person that could give Bible reasons for what she did, I was attracted to Christ. The fact that she had a basis for her decisions made a difference to me. The result was that, at twenty-four years of age, I put my faith and trust in Christ.

That young lady eventually became my wife, and now the Lord has given us five children, and we have served the Lord together for the past thirty-three years.

What a blessing it is to be used in the lives of others! Are you different in your purpose? Are you following Matthew 5:16 by letting your light shine before others and glorifying your Heavenly Father? If you are, others will be attracted to Jesus Christ through your life. I challenge you to read again the simple principles of being different on purpose from these pages. People around us are looking for answers. Do you have them? Are you ready to share them with others? Here's the plan—I Peter 3:15: *"But sanctify the Lord God in your hearts: and be ready always to give an answer to every man that asketh you a reason of the hope that is in you with meekness and fear:"*

CASE STUDIES

Case studies provide an opportunity to apply Scriptural principles to lifelike situations. Chapter Ten, "A Different Way of Handling Problems," summarizes ten key principles. In the following situations there will often be more than one *problem*, or principle violated, in each situation. Similarly, you should expect more than one passage of *Scripture* to apply, and there may be different elements of the *solution* to implement.

1: "Just Hanging Out"

It started out simply enough—just a bunch of guys camping out in the Linderman's den. We had more snacks than a small grocery store. Dad and Mom had given me a rough time about coming anyway since they didn't know the family that well. Honestly, I didn't know Larry's folks weren't going to be home. I know Mom and Dad wouldn't have let me come then.

Two hard-hitting war videos and three packages of Oreos into the evening, Larry slaps in another DVD movie. This one is no war movie... the only war going on was the one inside me. Larry smiles as the title, _____, flashes across the screen. A couple of my buddies look at me trying to cover up their own horror. Whatever decision I'll make now, I'll have to live with for a long time at school.

What is the problem?

What does the Scripture say?

Possible solutions?

2: "What, Another New Car?"

"Hey, John, did you notice who is driving a new car at church? Can you believe it, Jim and Joyce Smith! They just purchased a car a couple of years ago, and now another new one. And here I am still patching my '82 Olds together." It's interesting to me that Jim was just complaining about the high cost of Christian education last Sunday. If they are having problems paying their school bill, how can they afford a new car? Some people always want more.

What is the problem?

What does the Scripture say?

Possible solutions?

3: "The Hostess Party"

Have you ever been the hostess of one of those home sales parties? Sue reluctantly gave one for a friend to get points. She invited her mother, mother-in-law, and some friends and neighbors. Though she didn't know the lady that would be demonstrating the product, she knew the product was good and thought it would be a fun ladies' night out. As the demonstration progressed, the sales lady would occasionally drop inappropriate remarks. She was evidently trying to be funny, but no one was laughing. Sue was embarrassed and felt very frustrated. She wanted to jump up and tell that lady to pack up her wares and leave. She tried to ignore the problem and finished the party as though nothing were wrong. What could she have done?

What is the problem?

What does the Scripture say?

Possible solutions?

4: "Wanted: A Husband Who Leads"

Herb is a good husband and father. He works hard to provide for our family. His only problem is that he's so passive. He's just not being a leader in our home. Sure, he gives the kids plenty of attention—playing with them, buying them treats and bringing home surprises—but when it comes to correcting them, he leaves the discipline up to me. I wish he'd be a spiritual leader, too. He attends church faithfully, but when he's home, the only thing he does is lead in prayer at mealtime. We never have family devotions or pray together as a couple like many of my friends do. I've talked to him about doing a better job of leading, but it only turns him off. Am I asking too much of him to expect him to perform his God-given role?

What is the problem?

What does the Scripture say?

Possible solutions?

5: "You Know Chuck"

You know Chuck... always keeping things stirred up. Do you have a Chuck where you work? He gets quite a charge out of making fun of anything spiritual, and what a foul mouth he has! Sometimes I think he is harmless enough; no one takes him seriously. Lately, however, the things he says really trouble me. His talk about wild parties is quite the thing every Monday, and he has his opinion on everything. He knows that some of us don't like his vulgar language, but he doesn't seem to care. What do you do with a Chuck around? Any ideas?

What is the problem?

What does the Scripture say?

Possible solutions?

6: "Give Me a Break"

I consider myself a pretty good Christian—I am faithful to church, give pretty consistently, and even sing in the choir. You certainly can't say that about some members. I've even been thanked on occasion for my faithfulness. So why all the push about the special men's meetings beginning this year? It seems like Pastor expects more out of the faithful few each year. If it's not initiating men's meetings, then it's a push for visitation or another evangelistic campaign. I don't need to be preached at because others aren't faithful. Besides, Pastor says the family comes first. At least that's what he told me last year when I wanted to start a Monday evening gym night. "Monday night is family night," was his reply. Can't he just give me a break?

What is the problem?

What does the Scripture say?

Possible solutions?

7: "The New Kid"

Boy, he sure looks lonely over there eating lunch by himself. He does dress a lot differently than the other students. Someone said that he doesn't have a father, and his mother just moved here to live with her parents. That's a tough break for a junior higher. I've tried being friendly to him, but he acts like he would rather we leave him alone. I suggested to some of the guys in class that they invite him to eat with them, but they said, "And talk about what? He doesn't seem to be interested in sports. It's obvious that he has no school spirit. If he wanted to get in with the kids at all, obviously he should show up at some of the school events." They are right, I guess, but he surely does look lonely. Oh, well, he looks weird, too. Some people are just cut out that way, I guess. What would you do?

What is the problem?

What does the Scripture say?

Possible solutions?

8: "The Uncommitted Committed Teens"

As a Sunday school teacher, I'm really concerned about our young people. It just seems that they are not as committed as they used to be. Most of them are not showing up for visitation, but they always have time for their school activities. In fact, I was really upset last month when I had worked so hard planning our evangelistic gym night, only to find out at the last minute that the Christian school had planned an all night lock-in the night before. I'm certain that you know what happened. Most attended the lock-in, but were too tired to attend the activity the next night. Oh, yeah, a few of my so-called committed teens came to the activity, but only one brought a visitor. I talked to one of the other youth workers, and he agreed. We both get upset when Pastor praises these teens so much from the pulpit. Where is their love for the Lord? Where are the parents? What are their priorities? I told the youth pastor, and he said he will say something to them. I'm praying he really gives it to them. I know my Sunday school lessons are going to be on loyalty to the church. Maybe that will get them fired up for my next big activity.

What is the problem?

What does the Scripture say?

Possible solutions?

9: "She's Changed!"

"What happened to Chris over the summer? Does anyone know? She is really different from the way she used to be." Comments like these are heard all over the school. She spent a good bit of her summer with her father in another area of the country. I think everyone is a little surprised by how hard she looks. Well, not really hard, just different. You know what I mean. She was really spiritually tender last spring. She even attended class prayer meeting, but it's not what she's into now. She is not unfriendly, but I guess COLD would be the word that describes her now. I think it's just terrible that students lose their love for the Lord over the summer. Why can't people just keep growing? I asked her how her summer went, and she said, "OK," and went on. Maybe when school revival comes she will get straightened around.

What is the problem?

What does the Scripture say?

Possible solutions?

10: "Sick of It"

Whew, finally finished? It was one tough history test, all right. I had studied for hours and believed I had done pretty well, and with 10 minutes to spare I began to look over my answers when I saw Joel. There he was writing answers furiously from a small piece of paper. I am so tired of this. Why doesn't he just study like the rest of us? He has the brains and could make good grades on his own. But he is always copying homework, and I've had it. Wait until I tell the guys. I think they are sick of it, too. Why don't the teachers ever catch him? Don't they realize there is a problem? Why does this happen in a Christian school? *"Hey guys,"* I said as the bell rang, *"wait for me."*

What is the problem?

What does the Scripture say?

Possible solutions?

Appendix 2

PART 1: FOR HUSBANDS
SERVING MY WIFE

*Husbands, love your wives, even as Christ also loved the church,
and gave Himself for it. Ephesians 5:25*

- Make her coffee in the morning.

- Adjust the temperature a bit early, before she is up and around.

- Ask about her car (fix, clean, scrape the ice, change the oil).

- Volunteer to go to the store. Call from the store.

- Call during the day… for a good "no reason."

- Go directly home, and go directly to *where she is.*

- Stay in the kitchen during supper preparation.

- Be the first one to ask the questions.

- Answer the questions with no irritation or exasperation.

- Remember to ask what her schedule will be and specifically ask how it went at the end of the day.

- Take charge at the meals to see that the conversation is "building" not "ripping."

- Ask good questions about the children's schedules.

- Lead the way in complimenting.

- Do the dishes or clear the table.

- Take the children's practice schedule as a personal project.

- Do anything to help with homework.

- Read to the younger children. (tape your news program for viewing afterwards.)

- Put at least one child to bed on a regular basis.

- Turn down the sound or put down the print when she is talking.

- Be personally involved in regular Bible study.

- Handle the discipline whenever you are at home to do it.

- Skip a hobby session to do something she considers an emergency.

- Keep the phone by you… answer it.

- Command yourself into a decent mood.

- Initiate a family round table when the "same" problem keeps cropping up. Don't ignore patterns.

- Involve her in any discussion about major changes… without fail.

- Comfort her when she is down emotionally. Put your arms around her and silently hold her for a few seconds without lectures or put-downs.

- Correct her gently and tenderly.

- Watch that "edge" in your voice. Does your voice sweeten or harden when you speak to or about your wife?

- Do not respond defensively when she brings up a problem.

- If she considers something necessary, consider letting her spend the money on it.

- When she offends you, forgive her completely and immediately.

- Remember those positive, unique qualities that made you want to marry her. Dwell on them!

- Ask for forgiveness when you are wrong.

- Give her a soothing back rub a couple of times a week.

- Write and mail a letter to her. Tell her why you love her.

- Surprise her!

- Be her main protector, and do it biblically.

- Let her be the center of your attention in any crowd.

- Look carefully for any changes she has made about her appearance or the appearance of the house. Watch and note her efforts to please you.

- Be her best prayer warrior.

- Ask her about your habits that annoy her; then do away with them!

- Be a complete gentleman in the house—even to the point of table manners, dress, shaving, and sounds.

- Be loving toward her relatives. Serve them regardless of what you believe to be the level of their worthiness.

- Don't compare her to any other woman at any time in any way! Pointing out some ability she lacks or some characteristic, quality, or feature you prefer in reference to another woman is devastating.

- Thank her for everyday things that she doesn't even expect a "thank-you" for.

- Keep her informed of your schedule. Almost everything will affect her.

- In essence, she is equal to you in every way. Treat her that way.

- If she mentions being uncomfortable with the way another woman is acting toward you, listen and take action to distance yourself from that woman.

- Hold her hand in public.

- Remember anniversaries, birthdays, and other special occasions.

- Go shopping with her. Yes, shopping!

- Never belittle a feminine characteristic.

- Hear the logic behind the illogic.

- Never criticize her in public.

- Find a supper specialty and cook it regularly. Your best ability may be your ability to *drive* to a restaurant.

- Do the "honey-do" list.

- Read a book she recommends to you.

- Prove to her that she comes before business, children, your parents, your house, your hobbies and your games.

$\mathcal{A}ppendix$ 2

PART 2: FOR WIVES
SERVING MY HUSBAND

...and the wife see that she reverence her husband. Ephesians 5:33b

Reverence: *that she notices him, regards him, honors him, prefers him, venerates (respects) and esteems him; that she defers to him, praises him and loves and admires him exceedingly*

(Definition from The Amplified New Testament)

- "Love is kind." (I Corinthians 13:4)
    - o Practice acts of love and kindness.
    - o Speak in kind tones.
- Admire him.
    - o Make a list of his strong points under the topics of physical, intellectual, emotional and spiritual. Men like to be admired for masculine qualities. (Examples: leadership, athletic ability, intelligence, logic, and courage)
    - o Sincerely compliment him in these areas.
- Thank him specifically for all he does and is.
    - o His provision, his faithfulness to you and God, his giving spirit, his upkeep of the home and the car, his help around the house, his spiritual leadership, etc.
- Ask for his advice and follow it.

- Run errands for him cheerfully and remember his requests and hints.

  o Shampoo, favorite foods, desire to have a friend over for supper.

- Compliment him in public and to the children.

  o Never criticize, correct, or belittle him publicly.

- Be interested in his occupation and hobbies.

  o Ask questions and learn about them.

- Support and encourage his dreams.

  o Be loyal to him.

- Send him funny cards, thank you notes, romantic messages, etc.

- Pamper him.

  o Make his favorite foods, fix his coffee, give back rubs, whatever he likes.

- Take care of his clothes.

  o Clean, iron, mend, replace, dry clean.

- Sacrifice and plot to buy him unexpected gifts.

- Compliment and encourage his effort to grow spiritually.

- Let him know that you want to be with him and enjoy the time that you have together.

- Admire him in non-verbal ways.

  o Listen attentively.

  o "Light up" when you see him.

  o Wink at him from across the room.

  o Smile at him.

- Look nice for him and dress to please him (even around the house).

- Keep the romance going.

  o Hold hands, sit close to him, give him whole hugs, tease and flirt with him, etc.

- o Be the initiator sometimes in the physical relationship.
- o Enjoy lovemaking times and be sure he knows that you desire to be with him.
- Treat his family as special people.
  - o Remember birthdays, anniversaries, etc.
- Support and help him in areas that he desires to change.
  - o Diet, exercise, consistent family and private devotions.
- Ask him to pray for you and remember to pray for him.

Appendix 2

PART 3: FOR PARENTS
SERVING MY CHILDREN

My son, give me thine heart, and let thine eyes observe my ways.
Proverbs 23:26

- Ask them how you can serve them!

- Make their beds… occasionally!

- Try to find a unique—rather than a hated—way of waking them up, if waking them is your routine.

- Teach them how to have personal devotions. Ask often how they are doing in their devotional time. Purchase any materials they need to have a good "God and I" time.

- Have a relevant family devotion, even if it is short.

- Lead them to think through whether they have everything before they go out the door.

- For the younger ones, have games that only you play, so that they look forward to seeing you coming.

- Have an interest in their interests, even if it's not your interest.

- Take him to dinner or breakfast.

- Tell him you love him, even (or especially) during the teen-age years.

- Don't live your dream through them, but dream for them to please God.

- Comparison between your child and any other is devastating, not to mention wrong!

- When he makes progress, tell him. Bring out the trumpets. Don't ever say, "Well, it's about time!"

- Volunteer constantly to help him with his homework.

- Never let your TV show or newspaper stand in the way of eye, ear, and heart contact.

- Involve him in your relaxation or hobby.

- Take him, and him alone, on a ministry trip. Make it a memory of a lifetime.

- Tell him when you are burdened and ask him to pray for you. We're not here to teach him that there are no problems in life. We are to teach them the biblical handling of the problems that will come.

- Read to them from the time they are very young.

- When you explain, remember that this is his first time to hear the explanation. Go slowly. Watch the edge in your voice when understanding comes slowly.

- Cheer for the same teams, if possible.

Appendix 2

PART 4: FOR CHILDREN AND TEENS
SERVING MY PARENTS

Bathroom

- Get on a schedule and keep it.
- Volunteer to clean it; it'll make you appreciate Mom.
- Warn people when you must be "in" for a long while.
- Does Dad have a particular way to find the toothpaste?
- Where does Mom want the nylons?
- All the hot water? Come now!
- Rinse out bathtub after use.

Living Room/Den

- Finish homework before watching TV.
- Don't get a reputation as being hooked on TV beyond help.
- Treat the newspaper with care.
- Turn off the lights.
- Carry an "armload" with you when leaving.
- Give Dad and Mom "the" chair.
- Refrain from horseplay to prevent broken valuables.
- Treat stereo/tape player with care.

Kitchen

- Take out the trash—regularly.
- Come in 10 minutes early; ask to help.
- Help clear the table automatically.
- Load the dishwasher.
- Wash and dry the dishes.
- Have a specialty (i.e., spaghetti, salad, dessert) and volunteer to make a meal once a week.
- If Mom wishes to talk with you, don't make her do it long distance.
- Sweep the floor.

Bedroom

- Don't decorate it in an objectionable way.
- Find out the next day's schedule.
- Get an alarm clock. Use it!
- Don't let Mom have to call you; this includes Sunday morning.
- Never leave your bed unmade—ever.
- Know where dirty clothes go.
- Know where sweaty clothes go.
- Keep the room picked up.
- Keep the trash can emptied—clean it on occasion.
- Invite others in—don't make it a selfish retreat.
- When not dressing, keep the door unlocked and open for the most part.
- Use Scripture to remind you.
- Don't put up "keep out" or "I hate you" signs.
- Invite your parents in to pray with you over a particularly troublesome issue.
- Hang ups—you must have hang ups.

Morning

- Wake up without being called (alarm).
- Have "wake-up" devotions.
- Memorize a morning cheerfulness theme.
- Go to breakfast a few minutes early.
- Talk—be a human.
- Help clear the table.
- Ask Dad or Mom if he or she is expecting a rough day.
- Hug and kiss them—always treat it as if it were the last day.
- Tell them you love them.
- Be ready on time to leave for school.

Phone

- Don't ruin your testimony.
- Don't put parents on the spot for a split-second decision—give them time.
- Agree with your best friends about time limit—ask Mom—set timer.
- Don't shout at younger brother or sister—makes Mom & Dad hate the phone (or video or TV).
- Do homework first—make telephone time a reward.
- Read the signals (eyebrows, throat) but don't blame parents over the phone.
- Call home several times—for good reasons or for no special reason.
- Don't be disappointed if it is the neighbor or a church friend.
- Answer the phone politely—you are representing the family.

Car

- Return it with gas.
- Pick up paper and trash—vacuum.
- Armor All

- Wash it—bring it home washed.
- Learn to check the oil.
- Move the seat back.
- Insist that all passengers buckle up.
- Ask how much the insurance went up when you became a driver (Ask when your Dad is sitting down).
- Return keys to their proper place.
- Park the car where they want it.
- Drive safely; don't take chances.

Dating
- Don't get frustrated with the FBI—go quietly—turn yourself in! (who, what, where, when, how long?)
- Be proud of your parents—introduce them.
- Be early (getting ready & getting back home) "early 10 is the most important 10"
- Discuss date if that's what they want.
- Share your heart with them... what to look for in a date; qualities that are important to you; how Dad can help "bail you out" when necessary.

Yard
- Join parents if they have interest here (e.g., flowers).
- Mow it (the way Dad wishes).
- Keep it picked up.
- Rake leaves.
- Haul trash.
- Help an elderly neighbor.
- Help an elderly relative.
- Volunteer to help with the church lawn.
- Clip hedges.

Church

- Don't sit on the back row.
- Bring Bible without being reminded.
- Give your precious dollars.
- Be willing/able to share one way in which you can change.
- Sit with family at times.
- Don't criticize unless you have gone to the person.
- Help with meals—Sunday is generally a frustrating day for Mom.
- Help dress little brothers and/or sisters.
- Don't cut up with friends during the song service—it is an important part of church, too.

www.ingramcontent.com/pod-product-compliance
Lightning Source LLC
Chambersburg PA
CBHW070825100426
42813CB00003B/488